THE THREE R'S OF CHRISTIANITY

THE
THREE R'S
OF
CHRISTIANITY

Jack Finegan

JOHN KNOX PRESS • Richmond, Virginia

230
F494

154269

Library of Congress Catalog Card Number: 64-10078

Except where otherwise indicated, Scripture quotations are from the Revised Standard Version, copyright 1946 and 1952 by the Division of Christian Education of the National Council of the Churches of Christ in the United States of America.

© M. E. Bratcher 1964

Printed in the United States of America

9272 (20) D. 5791

Preface

In the theological thought of our time there has been a greater
interest in and, it is hoped, a deeper understanding of some of
the biblical doctrines concerning what God does for man, than
was the case in some earlier eras. This does not necessarily mean
that those who try afresh to understand these doctrines are completely pessimistic about man. It does mean that they are more
realistic, and perhaps humble, and realize that there are things
which man cannot do for himself. Thus there has undoubtedly
been a greater readiness than at some previous periods to listen
carefully to the message of the Bible about how God manifests
himself to man, endeavors to bring man back into a relationship
with himself from which man has departed, and sends Jesus
Christ to accomplish, at no small cost, this end. Biblical teachings about these several matters may be stated in doctrines of
revelation, of redemption, and of the Redeemer, and it is with
these doctrines that the present book is concerned. As in other
of my books which are intended to state theology in a way that
can be understood by the ordinary reader, so here too the attempt
is made to write plainly, yet not to lose the sense that it is with
great matters, indeed with vast mysteries, that we deal.

Jack Finegan

Contents

Part One:

REVELATION

I

The Word of God

The basis of theology is revelation. The question asked in Job 11:7, according to the American Standard Version, "Canst thou by searching find out God?" is clearly intended to elicit a negative reply. Man cannot hope by his own unaided effort to seek out and discover God. But God, according to the Bible, makes himself known, and this fact is the foundation of all theology.

In the Bible, from the first chapter of the first book on, this self-manifestation of God is frequently referred to with the statement that "God said,"[1] and in later books it is often declared, "Thus says the LORD."[2] Likewise there is frequent reference to "the word of the LORD,"[3] "the word of God,"[4] and "the Word."[5] It seems obvious that to affirm that God "said" and to speak of his "Word" is to use symbolic language. If the use of this-worldly figures of speech to stand for other-worldly matters is mythological, as in our time it is the fashion to call it, then this is the language of myth. But we cannot speak of matters which lie beyond us without using terms growing out of things present. Everything depends upon understanding what the mythical or symbolic language we use is intended to express.

THE MEANING OF "THE WORD OF GOD"

Our first question, therefore, is to ask what the term "the Word of God" says to us about the nature of God. For one thing it suggests that the nature of God is contemplative, that God is characterized by thought and wisdom and understanding. A word is the expression of an idea. Before it is an uttered sound it is a thought in the mind. Some people may seem to talk without thinking, but the wise man thinks before he speaks, and words are ordinarily, at least, the expression of what is already present in thought. Some people may think in profound abstractions or in mathematical formulas which go beyond words, but most of us use words in our thinking. In our ordinary experience, therefore, a word is an idea-conveying sound or group of sounds, and these may in turn be represented by a sign or group of marks. But back of the marks are the sounds and back of the sounds are the ideas. To say that God speaks and to talk of the "Word" of God is accordingly to be reminded of the thought of God. Indeed the Bible explicitly tells us that God is characterized by wisdom and understanding.

> "With God are wisdom and might;
>   he has counsel and understanding."[6]

> Great is our LORD, and abundant in power;
>   his understanding is beyond measure.[7]

It seems entirely reasonable to believe that God is by nature characterized by thought and understanding. It is by our own power of thought, such as it is, that we are able to trace out as much of the workings of God's universe as we are. But it is also convincing to think that God is characterized by wisdom precisely because our thoughts are insufficient to comprehend all of his ways.

> "For my thoughts are not your thoughts,
>   neither are your ways my ways,
>   says the LORD."[8]

In any serious intellectual pursuit we come to limits and boundaries. We find that our thoughts are insufficient to penetrate all mysteries, and there on the edge of greater mystery we feel ourselves in the presence of the infinite. In an extended poetic work descriptive of the great enterprise of science, Alfred Noyes has, in the following passage, expressed something of both sides of the matter:

Man is not exiled from this Majesty,
The inscrutable Reality, which he shares
In his immortal essence. Man that doubts
All but the sensuous veils of colour and sound,
The appearances that he can measure and weigh,
Trusts, as the very fashioner of his doubt,
The imponderable thought that weighs the worlds,
The invisible thought that sees; thought that reveals the miracle of the eternal paradox—
The pure unsearchable Being that cannot be
Yet IS, and still creates and governs all;
A Power that, being unknowable, is best known . . .[9]

The expression "Word of God" suggests not only that God is contemplative but also that he is creative. A word has a function in the making of things. Man gives constructive commands and things are done. This is a way the Bible speaks about the Word of God. He utters his command and it is done. As far as we now know, this conception of the creative character of the Word of God was first formulated by the Sumerian philosophers of Lower Mesopotamia long ago. Samuel Kramer, probably our leading authority in the interpretation of the ancient Sumerian literature, tells us that the early Sumerian thinkers conceived of creation as taking place by the command and at the word of the deities in whom they believed. So a doctrine was developed which, as he puts it, became dogma throughout the ancient Near East, namely, the doctrine of the creative power of the divine word.[10] Perhaps it was out of this Sumerian heritage that this idea was brought into our Bible, and there it is lifted up to its full meaning and set forth in its great sublimity, particularly in the first chapter of Genesis. "And God said," we read, " 'Let there be light'; and there was light," and similarly at his creative command there came into being the firmament, earth and sea, the sun, moon, and stars, fish and birds, the beasts of the earth and man.

As the psalmist sums it up, "By the word of the LORD the heavens were made . . ."[11] As Hebrews puts it, ". . . the world was created by the word of God . . ."[12]

It also seems reasonable to say that the nature of God is creative. This thought may be supported by the analogy of how man makes things. When we come upon an intricately contrived mechanism, we conclude that there is the thought of a maker behind it. Paley's watch long ago suggested to him the watchmaker. Even so this much more intricately contrived universe with all of its parts, including man himself, speaks of a Creator. Yet it is even more convincing to think of God as the Creator when we remember the contrast between his creative power and the fact that man never can really make any object in the sense of creating it. The most that man can ever do is to fabricate, to manufacture, to put together into new combinations things which already exist. It was, to be sure, sometimes the manner of primitive thought to consider that God created the world by molding and shaping material that was already there. Or Gnostic thought conceived that there were emanations proceeding from the divine being, each crasser and more material than the last. But the great sublimity of the biblical statement consists in its affirmation that God said and it was so. As Paul says of God, he "calls into existence the things that do not exist."[13] He is pure being who sustains in being that which has no power of being in itself.

God is contemplative and creative, and by the implications of the term "Word of God" he is also communicative. This, most of all, is what a word signifies. It is a medium of communication. It is a sound or group of sounds which carry from here to there through the air. Transformed into electronic impulses, they travel through the ether and make communication possible over great distances. Transformed into marks and signs on pieces of writing material, they may be sent afar or preserved for long periods of time. Even if the vocal mechanism which forms sounds and the aural mechanism which receives them fail, then the words may be transformed into signs which are made with the hands, or be represented by raised dots on stiff sheets of paper, and thus provide for communication. If, then, a word is most of all a means by which an idea is carried from one person to another, it must be that when the Bible speaks of the "Word of God" it is suggesting that it is the nature of God to be communicative. "The word of the LORD came," we read in the Bible, "to Nathan,"[14] "to the prophet Gad,"[15] "to Solomon,"[16] and to Elijah[17] and others. Concerning the declaration of the prophets that the Word of the Lord came to them, C. J. Wright says: "The Prophets meant by such statements that they believed God had made known to them, in the depth of their own mind, His very thought and purpose."[18]

And once again it also seems reasonable to believe that God communicates. We believe that God is personal and that man is made in his image; therefore personal communication between God and man is something to be expected. It is reasonable to accept as coming from God many things which are said in the Bible because they agree with the best that we can know from searching out the ways of the universe. But we are also convinced that we receive communications from God because what comes in the Word of God to man is often also something which disagrees with man's best thinking, which contradicts his own conclusions, which contravenes his ideas, and which commands him to do something which he does not want to do.

"Word of God" is a symbolic term, therefore, which suggests to us that it is the nature of God to be contemplative, that is, thoughtful, wise, understanding; to be creative, that is, to make the world by his very Word, to call into existence what is not in existence, and to sustain in being what has no power of being in itself; and to be communicative, that is, to speak to men, to send forth his Word to be received by his people.

THE RECEIVING OF THE WORD

Our next question, then, is as to how man receives the Word of God. If the Word of God has meaning for us, it must be that we receive it in the same manner in which we receive anything else that has meaning, that is, by reason. But, as Paul Tillich has suggested, we may distinguish two ways in which reason operates. For one thing, there is what we may call technical reason. This is reason as it functions in scientific endeavors and in many everyday considerations. Here reason works logically, empirically, analytically. This is necessary. This is important. This is fruitful. How much has been done by scientific thinking! Man has analyzed the elements and split the atoms. In fact, because this method has proven immensely effective, we modern people are sometimes obsessed by the technical use of reason.

But when we stop to remember, we realize that in the technical use of reason something is all the while eluding us. We look at a forest, and by technical reason we consider how many trees there are in it, how many board feet of lumber we may obtain from it, how much the logging operation will cost, and what profit we may expect from the enterprise. All of this is necessary and important, for we need wood to build houses and for many purposes. But when we look in that way there escapes us the thing which Joyce Kilmer saw when he looked at a tree and said, "Only God can make a tree." We look at a person and by technical reason we can consider a person analytically with great success. We can probably find out all of the constituent elements of the person. All of these elements can be listed in terms of chemical formulas. We can write a series of such formulas upon the blackboard and thereby completely and exhaustively describe everything that there is to that person—everything except what makes that person significant to us, everything except what makes that person our friend. I venture to think that no one ever fell in love with a chemical formula on a blackboard. Yet from the point of view of technical reason that is a complete description of a person. Something someway eludes us in this kind of operation of thought. We look at a sunset and we can view it by technical reason. We know about wave lengths of light, and we can study the sunset in these terms. But then something also still eludes us, something which I suppose John saw as he stood on the rocky island of Patmos off the coast of Asia Minor and watched the sun sink into the Mediterranean to the west of him. The sea grew calm at evening time, and the fire of the setting sun seemed to spread over the surface of the sea. In that sublime spectacle, as we may suppose, he caught a glimpse of "a sea of glass mingled with fire,"[19] which was to him a vision of eternity.

There must therefore be another way in which reason operates other than the way which we call technical. To use a word which is significant in present thought, this way may be called existential. This is the way reason operates when we confront the whole of reality with the whole of ourselves, and when we experience the great critical times of human existence. This is the way reason operates when man receives the revelation of the Word of God. Paul Tillich puts it like this: "Revelation is the manifestation of the depth of reason and the ground of being. It points to the mystery of existence and to our ultimate concern. It is independent of what science and history say about the conditions in which it appears; and it cannot make science and history dependent on itself. No conflict between different dimensions of reality is possible. Reason receives revelation in ecstasy and miracles; but reason is not destroyed by revelation, just as revelation is not emptied by reason."[20]

What is meant here may be illustrated by the sort of experience which Nathaniel Micklem has described in these words:

> I imagine myself climbing with a friend in a strange part of the country. I have plodded on through the woods and then among the dark crevasses, and then quite suddenly and quite unexpectedly I emerge upon a ledge or plateau in the open. The ground falls away before my feet, and spread out before me expands a panorama of sky and cloud and mountains and streams, and below me in the distance the quiet fields and the sea beyond. And I just gasp. For a minute or two neither of us says a word; then gradually we point to this or that; the scene begins to sort itself out in our minds; we commit it to memory; we shall be able to describe it to people when we get home—yet we shall never be able to describe it; it baffles all power and range of words. I offer this as a real parallel to what is revelation. In the first moment of wonder, when the glory of the scene breaks upon heart and mind,

there is, no doubt, an intellectual element, but it is sec-
ondary; it becomes predominant only when we try to
analyse, to remember, to report.[21]

Another illustration is to recall the well-known experience of
Brother Lawrence who said that he owed his conversion to seeing
a tree in the wintertime all barren and then reflecting that in
spring it would be clothed again with greenness. There before
him was a perfectly familiar object, an ordinary tree. One may
be concerned with such an object in the manner of technical reason; again sometimes in the great and critical moments of life
what we have called the existential reason may receive through
the very same object some communication from beyond. Thus
through nature, through history, or through human experience,
the Word of God may, upon occasion, come to us.

THE RESPONSE TO THE WORD

The response of man is also of importance when the Word of
God comes to him. In the experience of Moses as recorded in
the Old Testament, three aspects of that response may be seen.
It will be remembered that Moses saw a bush which was burning with fire, yet was not consumed, and that God called to him
out of the bush[22]—this presumably being the report of an experience with a phenomenon of nature which, perhaps in a manner not altogether dissimilar from the case of the tree and
Brother Lawrence, suddenly and unexpectedly became the vehicle of revelation. In the first place the response of Moses is a
feeling of reverence. At divine command he puts off the shoes
from his feet in token that he stands on holy ground. As the poet
puts it in well-known words:

> Earth's crammed with heaven,
> And every common bush afire with God;
> But only he who sees, takes off his shoes—
> The rest sit round it and pluck blackberries . . .[23]

In the next place the response of Moses appears in the resolution with which he returns to Egypt to the task which God has

laid upon him. He does not accept that task without protest, to
be sure, but he does accept it and does go to carry it out.

At yet a later time Moses again received the revelation of God,
this time upon Mount Sinai, where perhaps again striking phe-
nomena of nature were connected with the communication of
the Word. This time it is said that when Moses came back "the
skin of his face shone because he had been talking with God."[24]
Here is a part of human response which man presumably cannot
control, but which may also come to pass, namely, an experience
of reflected radiance in the face of the man who encounters the
Word. Thus reverence, resolution, and perhaps the reflection of
some new radiance, are possible aspects of man's response to the
receiving of the Word.

II

The Written Word

In the preceding chapter we have seen that the expression "the Word of God" says something to us about the nature of God. The "Word of God" is also a commonly used name for the Bible. An application of this term to the Scriptures is suggested in the Bible itself. Psalm 119 speaks repeatedly of the "word" of the Lord and in the same connection mentions God's law, testimonies, precepts, statutes, commandments, ordinances, and judgments. According to Jewish faith, the law and testimonies of God are written in the Scriptures. Therefore when the Psalm declares, "Thy word is a lamp to my feet and a light to my path . . ."[1] it is permissible to think of this statement as applying to the written Scriptures. Likewise Jesus, according to the seventh chapter of Mark, quoted from the Old Testament and then, referring to the alteration of the intent of Scripture in the interpretations of the Pharisees and scribes, reproached them for "making void the word of God" through their tradition.[2] Here again "Word of God" applies to what is written down in the Scriptures.

THE BIBLE AS THE WORD

In what way is it proper to call the Bible the Word of God? This term may be properly applied to the Bible because it is a record of inspired utterance. In 2 Timothy 3:16 it is declared,

"All scripture is inspired by God . . ." In the discussion in the preceding chapter we saw that the term "Word of God" suggests that it is the nature of God to communicate himself. The name for that communication in general is "revelation," the word which we employed in the foregoing chapter. The name for the same process as it relates to the written records of the Bible is "inspiration." Like revelation in general, inspiration in particular means God's communication of himself. That such a process has actually been involved in the writing of the Scriptures is affirmed in a well-known New Testament passage which has to do with that part of the Scripture known as prophecy. ". . . no prophecy," it is declared, "ever came by the impulse of man, but men moved by the Holy Spirit spoke from God."[3]

There are at least partial analogies to the divine communication even in other areas of human experience. While the work of science is predominantly in the area of technical reason, even there we hear of syntheses and creative perceptions which appear to those in whose minds they take shape to have been given to them, to have come to them from without. A classical example is the case of William Rowan Hamilton. He began to study mathematics at the age of twelve. His great discovery was quaternions. Of the methods of analysis involved here, it has been said that they represented as great an advance over the methods of analytical geometry as the latter were over those of Euclidean geometry.[4] The great discovery was made by Hamilton when he was walking over the hills of Ireland and was just crossing a bridge over a stream. In a letter written to his son on the 5th of August, 1865, he described what had happened: "An electric circuit seemed to close and a spark flashed forth, the herald (as I foresaw immediately) of many long years to come of definitely directed thought and work, by myself if spared, and at all events on the part of others if I should ever be allowed to live long enough distinctly to communicate the discovery."[5] So remarkable did the event seem to Hamilton even at the moment when it transpired that he could not resist the impulse to stop and cut his new formula on a stone of the bridge which he was just going over.

In the fields of literature and of art there are yet closer analogies. It may be remembered that William Blake said of his great poem "Jerusalem" that it had been given to him. "I have written this poem," declared Blake, "from immediate dictation, twelve or sometimes twenty or thirty lines at a time, without premeditation, and even against my will. The time it has taken in writing was thus rendered nonexistent, and an immense Poem exists which seems to be the labour of a long life, all produced without labour or study. I mention this to show you what I think the grand reason of my being brought down here."[6] When he spoke highly in praise of this poem, he felt that there was no lack of modesty in his doing so, since, he said, "I dare not pretend to be any other than the secretary; the authors are in Eternity."[7]

It is likewise known that Milton conceived his *Paradise Lost* as a whole before he worked it out in its details, and that he spoke of it as having been dictated to him, and called it the "unpremeditated song." Percy Bysshe Shelley, who cites this very example in his "Defence of Poetry," writes himself: "Poetry is not like reasoning, a power to be exerted according to the determination of the will. A man cannot say, 'I will compose poetry.' The greatest poet even cannot say it; for the mind in creation is as a fading coal, which some invisible influence, like an inconstant wind, awakens to transitory brightness."[8]

What is observable in the exercise of the poetical faculty is also to be seen in the arts. This, too, is noted by Shelley as he writes further: "A great statue or picture grows under the power of the artist as a child in the mother's womb; and the very mind which directs the hands in formation is incapable of accounting to itself for the origin, the gradations, or the media of the process."[9] If, then, even in ordinary life, people tell of such experiences in which something comes to them from beyond, we are better prepared to accept the statements of the biblical prophets who testify that something has been communicated to them. Amos says:

"The lion has roared;
who will not fear?

The Lord God has spoken;
who can but prophesy?"[10]

Jeremiah declares again and again, "The word of the Lord came to me,"[11] and it is fitting that Franz Werfel has written a penetrating life of this prophet under the title *Hearken Unto the Voice*.[12] From the voice which pursued him, Jeremiah sought to flee, but he could not. The voice of God sent Ezekiel to speak to a people who would not listen to him, and the Lord told him, ". . . I have made your face hard against their faces . . ."[13] That which came to the prophets was often something which they did not want to receive, something which went against their own will.

Indeed, as we stated at the beginning of this book, it is only if God does communicate with us that we can hope to have any knowledge of him, for we are assuredly not wise enough to find him out all by ourselves. As it is said in the book of Job, ". . . God is great, and we know him not . . ."[14] H. Wheeler Robinson puts it like this: "God in Himself must for ever be beyond the reach of human comprehension, or He would not be God . . . The only way in which we can know Him is by His willing entrance into our human experience, i.e. by some form of activity or manifestation which we *can* know. This is one of the cardinal truths of revelation . . . i.e. that the initiative is with God."[15]

Concerning the inspired message which we find in the Bible, we must say, however, that it is not only communicated but also that it is conditioned. It is conditioned by the people to whom and through whom it comes, and by the situation in which they are. It is obvious that it is communicated to a people who speak a given language—Hebrew, Aramaic, or Greek—and it is conditioned by that language. It is presumably conditioned also by the ethical insight and by the religious sensitivity of those to whom it comes. Writing of *The God Who Speaks*, Burnett Hillman Streeter says: "Suppose, then, He does at times act in some special way upon the consciousness of any individual, we should expect this action, not to supersede, but to stimulate his highest powers, and to result in an enhancement of his profoundest insights. At such moments the individual might rise far above the level at which ordinarily either he or his contemporaries live and think. We should *not* expect him always or entirely to transcend the limiting conditions—historical, psychological, or even ethical—of his time, his race, or his personal idiosyncrasy."[16] Likewise H. H. Rowley discusses the process of inspiration as seen in various examples in the Bible and then points out that these examples "illustrate the principle that inspiration came, not by the suspension of personality, but through the organ of personality; that the message it brought was never unrelated to the writer's own thought and outlook, but always closely related to it; and that the form into which he cast the message owed much to him, and was not, therefore a perfect Word of God." "Yet," Rowley continues, "in so far as it was the Word of God, it was of abiding significance."[17]

Thus, because inspiration comes from beyond, it always tends to transcend the immediate situation; but because it comes within a concrete situation, it tends to be limited by that situation.

Once again we may observe that that which is inspired in the Bible not only is communicated and conditioned but also is consistent with itself if it is true. How do we know that that which is inspired is true? Jeremiah spoke of contemporary prophets who perverted the words of the living God;[18] therefore some kind of test is necessary. In our modern environment we are tempted to answer that question by saying that the way to test revelation is to check it against the findings of science. But this would mean that the real authority is in science, and that means in the area of technical reason. Therefore we must not limit ourselves to the acceptance of only what science has proved to be true. We are also tempted to test revelation by reason. But then we are setting up the authority of rationalism as the highest court of appeal. May it therefore be that the test of revelation is its own consistency with itself? When the whole of what is communicated fits together, it is convincing. Thus Paul Tillich observes: "Every understanding of spiritual things . . . is circular," and therefore speaks of the "theological circle." In a theological system, he says, ". . . neither the introduction nor any other part . . . is the logical basis for the other parts. Every part is dependent on every other part." [19]

Thus far we have said that it is correct to call the Bible the Word of God because it is a record of inspired utterance. It is also proper to speak of the Bible as the Word of God because it is a record of divine action in history. In form the Bible is not only the transcript of a message but also the narrative of happenings. In fact there is approximately an equal division between message and narrative in the Bible. If, for a very broad generalization, we say that the books from Genesis to Esther constitute history, and Job to Malachi message, then the division is about half and half in the Old Testament. If we consider the foundations of our knowledge of the life of Jesus, we usually hold that the two oldest sources are Mark and "Q," the former a swift narrative account, the latter a hypothetical collection of sayings. In the balance of the New Testament after the Gospels there is the book of Acts which narrates history, and the apostolic writings which communicate a message. So the writing down of message and the recording of action are, broadly speaking, the two main things which are found in the Bible.

In its record of what happened, the Bible relates such events as these: Abraham left Mesopotamia and went to Palestine; Israel fled from Egypt, and while the army of Pharaoh was engulfed in the sea the erstwhile slaves went free; empires rose and fell, with the result that Jewish exiles were now carried away to weep by the waters of Babylon, and again were allowed to return to their homeland.

The Bible not only tells of such happenings as these but also tells something of what these events meant. It says that God called Abraham.[20] It declares that the Lord led those slaves out of Egypt by a mighty hand.[21] It explains that he used the nations as a rod with which to chastise his people, but that he was also perfectly able to cast the rod down out of his hand when it had done his work.[22]

If we ask why it is that both narrative and message are contained in the Bible, we may believe that it is because both of these are needed to convey God's communication to us. As men saw these events happening, they also heard the prophets speaking and declaring the meaning of what was transpiring. Sometimes events fitted together into wonderful patterns, and those who saw it were moved to cry, "This is the LORD's doing; it is marvelous in our eyes."[23] Sometimes events fitted together into terrible patterns, but even then the prophets were enabled to perceive some purpose of God there. Emil Brunner has commented on how it is that there is as much narrative as teaching in the Old Testament and how both are equally emphasized. Historical facts, he says, ". . . only became significant as the manifestation of divine mercy or of divine wrath through the word of the Prophet to the people; but the Prophets do not claim that these historical events only acquire their meaning as revelation through their prophetic word. It is not that they give meaning to history by means of their word, but that God gives them insight into the meaning of the event, which it already contains because God is within it."[24]

THE BIBLE AS OBJECT OF STUDY

Why must the Bible be seriously studied? From the foregoing discussion the answer to this question is obvious and may be stated very briefly. The Bible must be seriously studied because it is a human record which has to do with the divine Word. Because it is literature, it must be studied in a literary way. Because it came in various languages, we must know something of those languages. Because it is a historical work, we must study it historically. All of this study must be done honestly, with readiness for any finding, because here we are working on the level of technical investigation. On this level no particular finding, whether negative or positive, can destroy or establish the fact of the divine revelation which, as we have seen, lays hold upon us on a different level of apprehension. Nevertheless, since the revelation does come through human experience and human history, it is of importance to investigate that experience and history as thoroughly as possible. In actual fact it may be said, I believe, that the over-all trend in present Bible study is to recognize that biblical records correspond more closely with

actual happenings than was formerly thought. This is particularly true where the Bible is studied against the new background
being provided by archaeological investigation. William F. Albright gives this opinion and forecast: "As critical study of the
Bible is more and more influenced by the rich new material from
the ancient Near East we shall see a steady rise in respect for
the historical significance of now neglected or despised passages
and details in the Old and New Testaments."[25] But now and
always the Bible must be studied because it is a human record.

THE BIBLE AND FAITH

Why must the Bible be read with faith? To this question the
answer also seems evident from the discussion in which we have
been engaged. Only if, as we read it, some response of faith is
awakened in us is the Bible really to us the Word of God. There
is no particular importance to the claim that the Bible is the
Word of God as a record of inspired utterance in the past and
a record of divine action in the past, unless the message also
becomes a message to us, and the happenings become happenings to us.

Concerning the message of God in the Bible, Nathaniel Micklem writes: "God speaks to us through the Bible, not because
we can look up, as in an encyclopedia, what he has said, but
because, as we read and meditate upon the Bible, he speaks to
us directly through it."[26] Long ago Origen said that this would
happen as we read the Bible: "He who with diligent attention
reads the words of the prophets will from his very reading experience a trace and vestige of inspiration in himself, and this
personal experience will convince him that these are no complica-
tions of men, which we are firmly persuaded are the words of
God."[27] The message must speak to us, and only then can we
properly call it the Word of God for ourselves.

The happenings must in some manner happen to us. Only then
is the record of those happenings really the Word of God to us.
Rudolf Bultmann has emphasized this very strongly, particularly
with reference to the cross and the resurrection. Indeed when he
speaks of the cross he seems to refer primarily to the present

fact that the Christian dies with Christ, and when he talks of
the resurrection he seems to point primarily to the present fact
that the Christian rises to new life with Christ. Of the cross he
writes: "To believe in the cross of Christ does not mean to concern ourselves with a mythical process wrought outside of us
and our world, or with an objective event turned by God to our
advantage, but rather to make the cross of Christ our own, to
undergo crucifixion with him." [28] And of the resurrection he says:
"If the event of Easter Day is in any sense an historical event
additional to the event of the cross, it is nothing else than the
rise of faith in the risen Lord . . ." [29] Important as is the point
here made, it seems to be stated much too strongly by Bultmann,
and Helmut Thielicke seems justified when he criticizes Bultmann for really reducing cross and resurrection to present phe-
nomena. It is not, Thielicke insists, that the resurrection is a
mythological statement of the result of an encounter with Christ,
but rather that the resurrection is what makes possible and
creates an encounter with him. The statement of Thielicke himself seems to do better justice both to the present meaning and
to the past actuality of cross and resurrection: "As events, these
things—viz., dying and rising again with Christ—certainly have
their place in the New Testament message, especially as pre-
sented by St Paul, but only in the sense that we bring our existence into relation with what happened once for all in the history
of A.D. 1-30." [30]

That the bringing of our present existence into relation to the
message and the happenings of the Bible can have very practical
results may be seen, for one example in many, in the following
narrative. In Seattle, Washington, a man was at the end of his
resources. He had been sick for months. He was unable to hold
a remunerative position. He felt he had nothing to live for. He
was in desperation. He registered at a Seattle hotel and requested
a room as high up as possible. He was placed on the seventh
floor, and it was his intention to jump from the window of his
room. When he entered the room, however, he noticed a Bible
lying on the dresser. With idle curiosity, since after all he had a
few minutes to spare, he opened it and read a portion here and

there. Before he realized what was happening, he was reading eagerly. A year later he said: "I know what you mean when you say the Bible saves from suicide! That Bible showed me the folly of my sin. It also showed me the Savior who could give me a new life. That Bible is responsible for my being a Christian today." And the man who spoke those words was a smiling and radiant person, again going ahead in life with inner joy and peace.

III

The Word Made Flesh

Thus far we have seen that the term "Word of God" signifies that God communicates himself, and that to speak of the written Word is to think of the Bible as an inspired record of that communication of God to man. In what places, then, is the Word of God expressed?

WHERE THE WORD IS MANIFEST

Seeking an answer to the question just enunciated, we turn to the prologue of the Gospel according to John and find that, for one thing, the Word of God is expressed in nature. The prologue begins with reference to the Word, and then forthwith states that "all things were made through him."[1] We may expect, therefore, to find a manifestation of the Word in the natural world. This the Old Testament taught when it said: "The heavens are telling the glory of God . . ."[2] This Jesus assumes when he says, for example, that God "makes his sun rise on the evil and on the good, and sends rain on the just and on the unjust."[3] In the great uniformities of nature is shown the impartial benevolence of God.

Nevertheless, nature is not an entirely unambiguous expression of the Word of God. It is a support to our faith, but it is also a problem for our faith. The impartial processes of nature may seem to represent indifference instead of benevolence on the part of the divine Being toward man. The sparrow falls, the wind is not always tempered to the shorn lamb. A tempest comes out of the wilderness and falls upon the house where the children of Job are banqueting, and the destruction of his family in this act of nature poses a problem for this man of piety.[4] Nature is an expression of the Word but not an altogether unambiguous expression.

History is an expression of the Word of God. In the prologue of John it is stated: "The light shines in the darkness, and the darkness has not overcome it."[5] We may interpret this to mean that the light of the Word of God has been shining in the darkness of the history of the world. We believe, indeed, that it has thus been shining more and more. The psalmist calls upon us to praise God not only "in his mighty firmament," that is, in nature, but also "for his mighty deeds,"[6] and that is, for his works in history. In history we think we do see the light of the Word shining increasingly in the long evolution of life and society upon earth and in the expansion of the Christian church around the world. But the light has to contend against the darkness, and the darkness is an element of history as well as the light. History is the conflict of the two. "The time-process," writes H. Wheeler Robinson, "in which we are all agents, and not mere puppets, is the partial and confused working out of an eternal purpose."[7] Thus history is an expression, but not an unambiguous and fully clear expression, of the Word of God, and New Testament eschatology, as Reinhold Niebuhr puts it, "assumes that human history will be fragmentary and contradictory to the end."[8]

Again, the Word finds expression in and through personality. The Word, it is declared in the prologue of John, is the "true light that enlightens every man."[9] This light, it is evidently being said, is a light which shines in the inner nature of men. Wherever there is devotion to truth and beauty and goodness, the light is shining. It shines thus in many places all around the world. Justin Martyr says of Christ: "He is the Word of whom every race of men were partakers; and those who lived reasonably are Christians even though they have been thought atheists; as among the Greeks, Socrates . . . and among the barbarians,

Abraham. . . . and many others." [10] Nevertheless the realm of personality is also subject to ambiguity. It is the realm of truth and beauty and goodness. It is a place where the Word of God is influential and effective. It is also, however, an area which falls under the sway of the demonic. The inner world seems never to be all serenity and light. Sometimes it is turmoil and conflict, and is beset by dark forces. At worst, passions run riot here that make men behave worse than the beasts; and at best, the best people have a sense of separation from God, and the most high sensitivity to God may be coupled with the most keen awareness of sin. At the most, the realm of personality is still on the human level. We still stand here on the side of man rather than on the side of God. Thus even in the area of human personality the Word does not necessarily have full expression.

Among persons there is a special group of people in and through whom the Word finds expression. "He came to his own home," states the prologue of John concerning the Word, "and his own people received him not." [11] The reference is evidently to the Jewish people. They are a special people and constitute a special area where the Word of God has been at work in the world. The Bible history comes quickly to this people. It begins, as far as human beings are concerned, with Adam, who represents all mankind. Then it comes quickly to Shem, who is the eponymous ancestor of the Semites, and to Abraham, Isaac, Jacob, and the children of Israel. This is the people to whom the Lord says that he has chosen them "to be a people for his own possession." [12] Yet, though the Word has been specially active in the midst of the people of Israel, these people have not been altogether receptive to the Word. Their own prophets repeatedly tell them that they have failed in their covenant relation to their God, that they have failed to live up to the purpose which he has for them. For this reason the prophets are forced to focus their hope upon a "remnant" [13] and perhaps at last upon only a single representative of their people. As Tillich puts it: "The history of Israel shows that no group can be the bearer of the final revelation, that it cannot perform a complete self-sacrifice." [14]

If the Word truly finds expression in nature, history, person-ality in general, and one people in particular, but in none of these fully, then we are directed at last to the thought of a single person in whom it may be found in its completeness. It is the affirmation of the prologue of John that the Word did find such manifestation. In the climax to the series of statements which we have been studying, it is declared: "And the Word became flesh and dwelt among us . . ." [15]

The necessary movement of thought from expectation focused upon a people to expectation centered upon a person is illus-trated, it would seem, in the experience of the prophets. They had hoped that their people would do God's will, then they had directed their expectation toward only a remnant of the people, and finally they went on to picture the servant of the Lord. The servant songs of Second Isaiah begin as if they were descriptions of the people of Israel. It is Israel to whom the Lord says, "You are my servant, I have chosen you . . ." [16] But as the songs go on, increasingly the individual traits predominate in the description until at last we seem to be looking not at a whole people but at a single person who will indeed be the representative of that people, but who as a person can do what a whole people cannot do. We find ourselves looking at a person who was "a man of sorrows, and acquainted with grief," who "has borne our griefs and carried our sorrows," who "was wounded for our transgres-sions" and "bruised for our iniquities." [17] The analysis of the philosophical theologian comes to the same conclusion. Only in a person can the Word speak fully. Tillich writes: "The break-through and the perfect self-surrender must happen in a per-sonal life, or it cannot happen at all." [18] This, according to the New Testament, did happen in Jesus as the Christ, the Word made flesh.

Likewise the realization, indicated above, that the realm of personality in general is indeed illuminated by the Word but also beset by the forces of evil, leads to the hope for a person in whom the Word is wholly present. The analysis of this point and the statement of the corresponding New Testament doctrine have been put by Emil Brunner as follows:

A human being may be as moral and religious as he likes, he is still merely a man, and as such he has nothing to tell me about God. For either he merely tells me something which I can examine for myself afterwards, and then he is a "teacher," and stands on the same level as I do; the only difference between us is that he is a few paces further on. Or he may really communicate to me something of a real mystery of God: then he can only do this in virtue of a divine commission, thus it is not he who speaks as himself; indeed, it does not really matter to me *who* he may be at all. His word is a prophetic word. But there is a further possibility: He Himself may be in His own Person this Divine Word, coming from the realm which lies beyond all human possibilities. Then He cannot be man, a man like the rest of us, including the man of genius and the prophet, but He must be the Son of God, He in whom the word of revelation, the secret word in which God speaks His own Name, a human being, has actually become flesh: He is the Christ. Then He speaks and acts as God Himself, with divine personal authority, no longer in virtue of a divine commission, but in virtue of His Divine Being, as the Son, to whom the Father "has given to have life in Himself." This is the perfected Word, the one which has actually come unto us, the Word in which the divine truth and righteousness, which was separated from us by the great gulf made by the Fall, comes to us Himself and imparts Himself to us as truth, righteousness, life: the Word in which God gives Himself personally to us, because in the Word He is personally present, as the bridge over the gulf between us and Him, as the Mediator.[19]

WHENCE COMES THE IDEA?

If the belief that Jesus Christ is the Word of God made flesh fits into the whole circle of thought of our Christian theology, the tracing of the origin and development of the doctrine is not of the greatest importance. Nevertheless it may be worthwhile to ask briefly whence this idea came. Is this an idea that is explicable from the Old Testament and Judaism, or does it correspond rather with the conceptions of Hellenistic philosophy so that we must suppose it to have originated only after Christianity had moved out into the Hellenistic world? Does it fit with, or is it alien to, the idea of the Word which we have been tracing otherwise in the Bible? Although very different opinions have been expressed on the matter, we may venture to hold that this idea comes from the background of the Old Testament and of Jewish religious thought, and that we do not have to go into the Hellenistic world to understand its origin. This is at once suggested by the parallelism between the first chapter of John and the first chapter of Genesis. Genesis opens with the statement: "In the beginning God."[20] The initial affirmation of John is: "In the beginning was the Word."[21] This sounds as if the latter author were consciously patterning his phraseology after that of the former. Then in Genesis, as we have pointed out earlier in our discussion, we read repeatedly, "And God said." His Word, we are thus told, went forth to do his creative work. Similarly in John we read that all things were made through the Word, and that the Word became flesh and dwelt among men. It seems evident, therefore, that John is in the stream of thought which is found already in Genesis. Such a judgment has been held, for example, by C. J. Wright who emphasizes the Hebraic character of the prologue of John and says: "The author, in speaking of God's 'Word,' is not borrowing a speculative conception from Hellenistic philosophical thought. He is expressing his fundamental faith in the revealing activity of God throughout all history. He goes on to express his central *Christian* conviction when he declares that a historical person, Jesus the Christ, is the incarnate expression of this revealing activity of the Eternal God."[22]

It is certainly true that when Christianity went into the Hellenistic world it found there the idea of the Word, which in Greek was called the Logos. The Stoics taught that the Logos was the immanent reason of the universe. Philo, a Jew strongly influenced by Hellenistic thought, spoke of the Logos as an intermediate divine principle or being between the transcendent God and the natural world, and indeed spoke of many such logoi, using the plural of the same term. When Christianity went out, therefore, into the Hellenistic world, it found people who were ready to hear this idea that Jesus Christ was the Word made flesh, but it also found dangers to the doctrine, lest it be transformed into one of these other ideas already prevalent, namely, an idea of general reason, or an idea of an intermediate being, neither God nor man. Therefore Gustaf Aulén seems justified when he argues that the Christology of the ancient church did not, in fact, represent the Hellenization of Christianity but rather the defense of Christianity against Hellenization.[23]

In addition to the question of whether the doctrine that Jesus Christ is the Word made flesh is explicable against a background of Judaism or Hellenism, it may also be asked whether the idea is congruous with the teachings of Jesus or must be attributed only to the thought of his disciples. One of the most radical reconstructions of the life of Jesus presently available is that of Rudolf Bultmann, who sees Jesus as the proclaimer of an eschatological message of the reign of God which is even then breaking in. What is the evidence that the climactic event of all the ages is then beginning to take place? According to Bultmann, it is basically Jesus himself in his own person who is the sign of the time.[24] That Jesus thought of himself in the christological terms soon employed by the earliest church of him, Bultmann does not, however, believe. But another study of the life of Jesus, that of William Manson, with which the thought of the present writer would be in better agreement, finds that the extraordinary sense of mission of Jesus did take form in his mind in the concepts of the Christ, the Son of God, the Servant of the Lord, and the Son of Man.[25] As a single example of the evidence which must be weighed, we may recall that in what is probably our very oldest source of the sayings of Jesus, the hypothetical document lying back of the sayings found in common in Matthew and Luke, is found the statement of Jesus, "All things have been delivered to me by my Father; and no one knows the Son except the Father, and no one knows the Father except the Son and any one to whom the Son chooses to reveal him."[26] Such important evidence makes it seem very probable that Jesus did, in fact, speak of his own special relationship to God. Regardless, however, of how any specific historical question is answered, Christian faith does recognize that the life of Jesus was eschatological event and revelatory event. Therefore the doctrine of John that Jesus Christ was the Word made flesh is both justifiable and necessary. Emil Brunner puts it like this: "The Gospel of John, with the preaching of Saint Paul behind it, is the chief book in the New Testament which makes explicit this implicit meaning of the confession of Christ; this book gives full value to the assertion: He Himself is the revelation. . . . The self-affirmations of the Johannine Christ state explicitly what the historical Jesus *is*, even though, literally, they are not the actual words of the historical Jesus."[27] And C. J. Wright says: "Jesus is 'the incarnate Word' because He knew Himself to be the unique Son. . . . Thus the author's [i.e., John's] declaration that 'the Word became flesh' is really the declaration of the whole mind of Jesus Himself."[28]

THE MEANING OF THE DOCTRINE

What does it mean that the Word became flesh in Jesus Christ? This general question we may break down into several more specific interrogations, and in regard to each adduce some comment from Christian theologians who have pondered this matter deeply. Is the incarnation, we may ask first, a matter of substance or essence? Should we consider that some mysterious physical substance is involved when the Word becomes flesh? Hardly. Shall we consider that it is the essence of God which is involved? Yes, surely. This is, indeed, the way in which the matter was formulated in the creeds of the early church. The Son, it was declared, was of the same essence with the Father. Now what is the essence of God? Aulén is surely right when he says that the essence of the Father is his loving will.[29] Therefore the incarnation in Jesus Christ must mean the embodiment in him of the same loving will which is the loving will of God. As

Luther said, "We find the heart and will of the Father in Christ."[30]

Is the embodiment in Jesus Christ of the loving will of the Father a human achievement or a divine act? A possible approach to the answer to this question is suggested by Donald M. Baillie in his book *God Was in Christ*.[31] There he draws upon the general paradox of grace which is so generally understood by humble Christian believers. It is the paradox which may be seen in a well-known statement by Paul. "I worked harder than any of them," writes Paul. When we recall the travels, the shipwrecks, and the labors of the Apostle, we would readily agree as to the surpassing magnitude of his endeavors. He has no sooner said these words, however, than he corrects himself: ". . . though it was not I, but the grace of God which is with me."[32] Paul exerted himself to the utmost, yet in fact it was God who did everything in him. And Baillie lifts that same principle up to application to the incarnation where the human achievement is the divine act, so that the statement of Jesus given in John 8:29 may be taken as literally true: "And he who sent me is with me . . . for I always do what is pleasing to him."

Is this fact of the Word's becoming flesh a matter, then, of two persons or of one? Here we may recall how another writer of our time also draws upon Paul for a clue for the elucidation of a profound matter. Nathaniel Micklem writes of Jesus Christ:

> It is the traditional doctrine of the Church that he is both God and Man, and theologians have attempted to give some account of the God-man. All their constructions seem to me to be open to grave objection and to be unintelligible in the end. I have no theory to substitute for theirs. But we understand Paul when he says, "It is no longer I that live, but Christ that liveth in me,"[33] and we do not ask how anybody can be both Paul and Christ, for we know from experience that one person can indwell another without destruction of the other's personality. When we try to describe what Jesus of Nazareth was, it seems necessary to say that the in-dwelling of the Spirit

of God, which in us is so partial, intermittent and imper-
fect, was in him whole, continual and complete. He was
himself, but he was the Spirit of God incarnate, he was
God himself made manifest in a human life.[34]

It is then a matter of history or of faith when we look to Jesus
Christ as the Word made flesh? As if in answer to our question,
Emil Brunner writes: "Faith never arises out of the observation
of facts, but out of the Word of God. This Word of God, however, has certainly come 'into the flesh,' and is thus connected
with observation. It is therefore just as false to maintain that
faith is born out of the historical picture of Jesus as it is to claim
that it can arise apart from the picture of Jesus altogether.
Rather faith arises out of the apostolic testimony to Jesus, or
out of the witness of the Church, which always includes the
picture of Jesus."[35]

And once again, in our series of questions about the meaning
of the fact that the Word became flesh, we ask whether a belief
in some form of pre-existence is involved. "In the beginning was
the Word," states the prologue of John, "and the Word became
flesh and dwelt among us." This "was written," says C. J. Wright,
"by an author who believed, not in the pre-existence of Jesus,
but in the Eternity of the Word of which Jesus was the incarnate
expression."[36] The eternal Word came into time in the human
life of Jesus. And when the swift days of this brief human life
were over, he who had offered himself completely to the doing
of the will of the Father, and had gone even unto the cross, went
on through the resurrection to be forevermore at the right hand
of the Father—even he, the man Christ Jesus.

IV

The Word of Preaching

In the preceding chapters we have seen that the Word of God is the whole creative, communicative activity of God. The written Word is the record of that communication, characteristically stated by the prophets in the form, "Thus says the LORD."[1] The Word made flesh is Jesus Christ, who characteristically speaks with personal authority, "I say to you."[2]

HOW SHALL THE WORD COME TODAY?

The further question which we must now discuss is as to how the Word of God shall come to the world today. Doubtless the Word will continue to come through the awareness of men of the continued creative, sustaining, and communicative activity of God. Doubtless the Word will continue to come as we read the written records of the inspired prophets and, reading, experience, as Origen said, some trace and vestige of inspiration in ourselves which convinces us that this is indeed God's Word that is speaking to us.[3] Doubtless the Word will come to the world through the hearing of the words of Jesus Christ and the receiving of them with faith. But precisely at this point we come to the matter with which we are now concerned. The inescapable logic of the matter has been followed through by Paul in a striking series of interrogations in the tenth chapter of Romans. Having established from prophetic testimony that "every one who calls upon

the name of the Lord will be saved,"[4] he then launches into his
series of questions and makes the two central ones these: "And
how are they to believe in him of whom they have never heard?
And how are they to hear without a preacher?"[5]

If we take seriously the doctrine that the Word became flesh
and dwelt among us in Jesus Christ, then we take seriously the
fact that the eternal Word found manifestation within the limitations of human life, and those limitations are very narrow, both
as regards space and as regards time. Jesus lived in Palestine,
rarely going outside the borders of that land, and it is a small
country, one hundred fifty miles from north to south, forty miles
across. He lived within the limits of the span of human life
which at best is brief and fleeting, and in his case it was a trun-
cated span, cut off in the early thirties. If, therefore, anyone
beyond that narrow area and beyond that brief time is going
to know anything about this climactic expression in human history of the Word of God, it can only be if someone tells somebody else about it. If the Word of God is his whole communicative activity, and the word of the prophets is, "Thus says the
LORD," and the word of Jesus Christ is, "I say to you," the word
of the Apostles is what we find in 1 John 1:3: ". . . that which
we have seen and heard we proclaim also to you . . ." Given the
facts which we have considered thus far, the word of preaching
then becomes the inescapably necessary mode of making known
that which has come into the world in Jesus Christ.

This word of the Apostles was first of all the word of eyewitnesses: ". . . that which we have seen and heard we proclaim
also to you . . ." Those who saw and heard had to tell others,
otherwise no one else would have known what had transpired. If
we may suppose that 1 John was indeed written by John the
Apostle, then we have in it an example of such testimony; if the
author was not himself an eyewitness, he still feels that he is
communicating that which comes from eyewitnesses. Assuredly
at many places in the New Testament we have eyewitness-
testimony, and throughout we have a report which rests back at
last upon what came from the original eyewitnesses. But the very
fact that the original witness had to be communicated through a

series of transmitters of it shows that it was possible for the word of preaching to be passed on from those who were eyewitnesses to those who had not been eyewitnesses but who, having received the word, could carry it on to the next person. Timothy, for example, was one of these, for he assuredly could not have been an eyewitness, yet to him came the injunction, "preach the word."[6] Thus the word of preaching is handed on from one to another, that it may be carried to the whole world. This handing on of the apostolic word from one who tells it to another who may tell it is, it would seem, the very essence of the apostolic succession.

Now let us notice in regard to this apostolic word which is the proclaiming to others of what has been seen and heard, how strongly the Apostles concentrated upon doing exactly this thing. In the sixth chapter of the book of Acts we read about the time when the activities of the church were becoming more manifold, even as the necessary undertakings of the church have continued to increase in manifoldness ever since. In the face of this situation the Apostles resolved to devote themselves "to prayer and to the ministry of the word."[7]

Also we may notice that as time went on there was a measure of differentiation in this apostolic work. We see this, for example, in the fifteenth chapter of Acts where Paul and Barnabas are at Antioch and we read that they were "teaching and preaching the word of the Lord."[8] This is the major twofold differentiation in the communication of the Word in the apostolic ministry: preaching and teaching. There is a reflection and a deposit of this differentiation throughout the New Testament records. To designate these two main parts of what is found in the records of the New Testament it is now customary to use two words out of the Greek New Testament in direct transliteration. The first of these is *kerygma*. This is that which is proclaimed. The kerygma is the proclamation and, as it is recorded in the New Testament, it is the deposit of the preaching activity of the Apostles.

The kerygma may be seen in the report of the sermons of Peter in the early chapters of Acts, and also in the record of some of the sermons of Paul in the same book. There seems to be a recurring pattern in the proclamation of the early Apostles. A summary of it might be something like this: Jesus of Nazareth did mighty works and wonders. He suffered as the prophets foretold. He was crucified by God's will. Afterward God raised him from the dead and he appeared to the Apostles. They are his witnesses. As Lord and Christ he is at the right hand of God and will come again to judge the world. Therefore men must repent and be baptized and they will receive the gift of the Holy Spirit.[9] This same kerygma, it may be recognized, was also amplified in the narrative of the Gospels. The Gospels tell these very events at greater length. This was the proclamation. This was preaching in the early church.

The other part of the differentiated ministry of the Word was teaching. It is now customary to use the transliterated Greek word *didache* to refer to the early Christian teaching and to the deposit of it in the New Testament. The Gospels and Letters of the New Testament contain didache as well as kerygma. For the so-called "Synoptic" record of the life of Jesus which is contained in the Gospels according to Matthew, Mark, and Luke, it is considered that the Gospel according to Mark is a fundamental source, and Mark is essentially a swift narrative corresponding to the proclamation. But another fundamental source, it is commonly believed, was a collection of sayings of Jesus (technically known as "Q"), and this collection was evidently made for the purpose of instruction. The First Letter of Peter, which may come from the Apostle himself, contains in its first chapters doctrines which are similar to those of the speeches of Peter in Acts, and then in the latter part contains instruction in the nature of Christian life and the duties of Christian living. Paul regularly begins his Letters with doctrinal affirmation but as regularly goes on to practical exhortation and instruction. So it was both preaching and teaching which from a very early time constituted the twofold ministry of the Word.

Such preaching and teaching appears to have been not necessarily only the communication of duly authorized and appointed personnel but also the communication that was carried on by any and every faithful, witnessing Christian. To realize the importance of this fact one has but to remember, for example, that before Paul ever began to preach and to teach, as we have just seen him doing, it was an ordinary and otherwise unknown member of the church at Damascus, Ananias by name, who went to him and spoke the words through which Paul was set upon this pathway of service.

This, the preaching and the teaching of the Word, is being continued until today. This is the way the Word is to continue to come to the world. This is a ministry which has been emphasized in the Protestant church through the years. Indeed, it is often thought that the pulpit may well be placed to one side to make it perfectly evident that the speaking one is in nowise pointing to himself but is pointing to that which is central, namely, to the table and to the cross of the Lord, but the word of preaching and teaching continues to be uttered in the churches and to be indispensable. In his survey of "The Onward March of Christian Faith," Paul Hutchinson wrote thus of the Protestant church: "When . . . the Protestant enters his church, while there may be quite an elaborate ritual centering on the service of Holy Communion, most typically he is waiting for that moment in the service which was the highest of moments to Luther, Calvin, Knox, and all the other great Reformers—the moment when the minister enters the pulpit for the preaching of the Word in the form of the sermon. The sermon is the climax of Protestant worship, though too often," Hutchinson added in trenchant fashion, "the feeble capacities of the preacher make it anticlimax."[10]

WHY IS PREACHING FOOLISHNESS AND WISDOM?

Preaching is a way in which the Word of God is to come to the world today. But did not the Apostle Paul call the word of preaching both foolishness and wisdom? The statement of Paul, just mentioned, is found in 1 Corinthians 1:21 where, according to the King James Version, he speaks of "the foolishness of preaching" or, according to the Revised Standard Version, "the folly of what we preach." The words "foolishness of preaching" suggest that the very method of preaching is foolish. Indeed must it not sometimes seem impertinent that one person should stand and speak to many? Must it not sometimes seem presumptuous that the same person should stand in the same place week after week and perhaps year after year and talk to the same people on the same subject? Must it not even seem dangerous? James reminds us that the tongue is a dangerous instrument, and he warns his brothers that not many of them should become teachers.[11] Must it not seem even contradictory that a human being should speak about the Word of God and speak the Word of God?

But according to the doubtless preferable translation found in the Revised Standard Version, it is "what we preach," that is to say, the very content of preaching, which seems like folly. Paul goes on to explain that the message of preaching is "Christ crucified" and that this is "a stumbling block to Jews and folly to Gentiles."[12] That the preaching of the crucified Christ was foolishness to the Greeks is most vividly illustrated by the experience of Paul at Athens, the very center of Greek culture, where the Apostle found it extremely difficult to obtain a serious hearing. That the preached message was not readily acceptable or understandable among the Greeks means that it is an offense to rationalism for, above all, the Greeks were people of rational thought. The message of preaching is not primarily rational or logical. It is not something born of human wisdom which we have to say. It is not logical that Jesus should have had to die. Rationalism considers him a great teacher and any great teacher should have lived as long as he could to teach as much as he could. It is not logical that the death of one man should be of unique significance. Rational thought would consider such a death as one illustration of the general law of sacrifice which might as well be illustrated in any one of many other places. It is not logical that God should be uniquely present in one particular event. Rational thought traces evidences of God's work everywhere and finds it difficult to think of one particular happening as decisively important.

That the message of preaching was also a "stumbling block" to the Jews means that it is an offense to moralism, for the Jews represented the highest type of moral activity and endeavor. Even until now, for the most part, the Jewish people have not been able to see that Jesus is the Christ, and moralism must evidently always be offended by the Christian gospel. Moralism expects adherence to established norms and Jesus contravened most of the accepted rules of his day. Moralism anticipates an outcome in life that is in line with conduct, but the result of the life of Jesus appeared to be personal disaster rather than benefit for himself for all his good deeds. Moralism means an endeavor to achieve salvation by our own righteousness but, as understood by Paul, the gospel declares that we do not attain salvation by our own righteousness but by the grace of God through Christ which we accept in faith. Therefore the word of preaching must always be an offense to moralism as to rationalism, and must often seem like foolishness and like a stumbling block to the world.

Yet the crucified Christ is, as Paul goes on to say, "the power of God and the wisdom of God," and the very "foolishness of God," as he also declares, "is wiser than men, and the weakness of God is stronger than men."[13] In all preaching which truly proclaims Christ there must therefore be power and wisdom beyond what is measurable by human standards. There is indeed power in the method of preaching. As defined by Phillips Brooks in the classic statement which has been repeated so often from his Lyman Beecher lectures, "Preaching is the communication of truth through personality." When this has been true, as it so often has been in the case of so many simple and humble exponents of the Word, how effective it has been. In about the year 1212 John of Bologna listened to Francis of Assisi preach and left a record of what he heard and saw and of what a deep impression it made. He went, he says, expecting to hear from so famous a man a very great outpouring of oratory, but when he got there he found that Francis spoke quietly and colloquially. When Francis had finished, John of Bologna was astonished by the fact that the crowd were all weeping, and men who would not have hesitated to shed each other's blood fell upon each other's necks and forgave past enemies. When Francis left the place that afternoon, thousands of people knelt down to kiss the hem of his frayed brown robe as he passed.

There is power in the method of preaching and there is also wisdom in the message. The fact that the word of preaching was foolishness to Greeks and a stumbling block to Jews means this. It means that we do not have to be wise in order to accept it. If we had to be wise enough to understand God, who could ever do that? In fact simple man and savant are alike at the foot of the cross. More marvelous still, we do not have to be good to receive this word. If we had to be good, good enough to stand up in our own righteousness in the sight of God, who could ever do that? But it is the message of the apostolic word that man does not have to be that good by his own achievement, that in fact he cannot be, and that he has only to receive the goodness of God which is communicated to him through Jesus Christ. So the word of preaching is indeed a communication of the wisdom and of the power of God.

WHO IS SUFFICIENT?

And now yet another question arises in relation to the preaching of the Word and that is, "Who is sufficient for these things?" This is the question which Paul asks in 2 Corinthians 2:16 out of his own affliction and anguish of heart, out of the realization that the impact of his ministry upon men has seemed both like death and like life. Who, indeed, is sufficient for this ministry of the Word, for this communication of the Word of God in preaching and in teaching? For a work such as this, it will surely be agreed, only one who seeks the best possible preparation that he can obtain for it will be as adequate as he should be. "The proper education of young men devoted to the ministry of the word," wrote Alexander Campbell, "is on all hands confessed to be a matter of unspeakable importance."

But beyond that, only one who knows that he is insufficient will be sufficient for this task. Paul Tillich has written: "No minister should claim more than his intention to speak the Word when he preaches. He never should claim that he has spoken it or that he will be able to speak it in the future, for, since he has no power over the revelatory constellation, he possesses no power to preach the Word. He may speak mere words, theologically correct though they may be. And he may speak the Word, though his formulations are theologically incorrect. Finally, the mediator of revelation may not be a preacher or religious teacher at all but simply someone whom we meet and whose words become the Word for us in a special constellation." [14]

And only he will be sufficient whose sufficiency is in some wise supplied by God. This is what Paul said in conclusion of his line of thought on this subject: ". . . our sufficiency is from God, who has qualified us to be ministers . . ." [15]

So it is that by the grace of God the Word which was passed on from one to another in apostolic days continues to be passed on and to spread in wonderful ways. It is related of Henry Ward Beecher that on one Sunday when he was still a young minister he was to engage in an exchange of pulpits. He rode out through the country across drifts of snow to the small country church where he was to speak. He went in and there was no one there. He took his place in the pulpit and one man came in and sat down in a back seat. The young minister wondered what to do but he decided to conduct the service in regular order and this he did, from beginning to end, preaching a sermon as earnestly as he could. After the benediction he went to the back door to greet the single auditor, but the man had already slipped out and gone. Twenty years later Dr. Beecher alighted from a vehicle in another village and a gentleman, whom he had never seen before as far as he could recall, came up and spoke to him and called him by name. "I do not remember you," said Beecher. "I suppose not," said the stranger, "but we spent two hours together in a house alone once in a storm." "I do not recall it, sir," was the reply; "pray, pray, when was it?" "Do you remember," asked the man, "preaching twenty years ago in such a place, to a single person?" "Yes, yes," said Dr. Beecher, taking his hand, "I do indeed; and if you are the man, I have been wishing to see you ever since." "I am the man, sir," he replied, "and that sermon saved my soul, made a minister of me, and yonder is my church. The converts of that sermon, sir, are all over Ohio!"

Part Two:

REDEMPTION

V

The Plight of Man

In the preceding section of this book we have studied the fact of revelation, which is the basis of theology. Now we turn to the major concern of theology—the redemption of man—and, in the remaining two sections, we will consider what redemption is and what is the work of the Redeemer.

Man needs redemption. The present state and condition of man are, it is generally agreed, not all that could be desired. There are different ways of saying what the problem is and what is to be done about it. Perhaps each of several ways is true on its own level, and all are necessary for a complete statement.

IGNORANCE

The problem of man is often said to be that of ignorance. This was the way the Greeks looked at the matter. The Greek philosopher Socrates believed that the first step in self-development is for a person to realize his own ignorance. Therefore he went around asking people questions. People would try to answer these questions and when they did so they would realize how little they knew. Most of them thereupon became very angry with Socrates and, as a matter of fact, people such as this finally accomplished his death. Some, however, upon being confronted by the penetrating questions of this philosopher, would realize how little they actually knew and then would try to think and to learn. Socrates also believed that the second step in self-development is to know what is good. It was his conviction that if one knows what is good for one, one then cannot help doing it.

As far as its general philosophy is concerned, modern science may be thought of as having this same outlook upon the problem of human life. Science generally feels that people are ignorant about things and that the necessary procedure is to learn about the things concerning which we are ignorant. Mankind may be thought of as being similar to a child growing up. A child gets hurt many times because he does not know all about things. He does not realize that fire will burn, and accordingly he gets burned. The only solution for these difficulties is for the child to gain experience and through the experience to obtain knowledge and thus to be able to manage his life more successfully. Even so in the childhood of the race, mankind is oppressed by darkness, fear, and superstition. Only as mankind gains knowledge does it become possible for man to be unafraid, strong, and happy.

That there is a great deal of truth in this analysis of the situation all of us will surely agree on the basis of our own experience. We know how many times we have had difficulty because of our ignorance. We often say, "If I had only known." We feel that if we had known better, we would have done better.

This analysis—of what the difficulty is in man's situation—points to education as the answer to the difficulty. Education includes study and research. Accordingly it means penetrating areas where formerly there has been darkness. Education also provides a technique for transmitting the accumulated knowledge of the past. Thus it is not necessary for us to go back and repeat all the experiments that have been done before. We are able to take advantage of what has been learned in many previous centuries. This undertaking of education is a major enterprise in our time. Most families which have children are heavily involved in it—they make it a very important part of what they are trying to do, to provide the opportunity of schooling for their children. In almost every community in our states and in our nation, education is valued highly, and a great deal of effort and a great deal of our resources are devoted to it. We also regard with much admiration the devotion of scientists, working year after year in their laboratories in the pursuit of truth, and the effective service of teachers, guiding the young into the riches of knowledge. Education must assuredly be accounted by us all as a great hope of the world. Some years ago, facing the danger of war, it was remarked that there was "a race between education and catastrophe." Such a race may be said to be going on all the time. Education is extremely important and constitutes a very significant way of dealing with the problem of man's life, insofar as man's life is not yet satisfactory and successful.

This is, however, not all that there is to the problem of human life or to the answer. Much as we realize the danger of ignorance and the contributions of education, we must also recognize that education, in and of itself, does not always mean goodness or happiness. The educated criminal is a more dangerous criminal. A scientific war is a worse war. As a matter of fact, when we are most fearful of the terrors of an atomic conflict, we may almost find ourselves wishing we were back in the earlier days when the only weapons available were broadswords or perhaps only the bow and arrow. See what knowledge has done for us! The more we have learned, the more we have come in peril of our very lives. Education has not always preserved nations from disaster. It was a nation which had the most renowned universities in the world, which some years ago fell under the sway of a dictator whose domination was afterward recognized to be very harmful. An individual man may know about the effects of alcohol upon the human brain, and yet allow himself to become an alcoholic. A man may know much about the effects of drugs, and yet become a drug addict. In addition, therefore, to the foregoing analysis of the problem and indication of a solution, it seems necessary to ask if there is any other level upon which we may raise the question of man's state.

MALADJUSTMENT

Another way of describing the unsatisfactory situation of man is to say that he is unorganized or badly organized. This analysis would seem to be that which was held by the ancient Romans. They believed that the world needed the Roman Empire, and they seem to have believed that the world would be saved by the Roman Empire. The Roman emperors were often hailed as divine saviors. When they came to the throne it was as the advent of a messiah. The Empire, indeed, did bring wonderful organization to the ancient world. It provided laws which are still basic to our own system of law. It brought order, security, roads, possibilities of intercommunication, and many other benefits.

The social sciences and psychology today would seem to agree with this analysis of man's difficulty as essentially that of maladjustment, or lack of adequate and proper organization. In the development of life upon earth, the movement has been from one-celled animals to more complex organisms. In the evolution of society, we have moved from the tribe to the city, the state, the nation, and the empire, and now at last we catch at least a glimpse of the possibility of a United Nations. Lack of proper and sufficient organization would seem to be what is holding man back.

The solution indicated, therefore, is organization. We all believe in this. We recognize the need for integration in personal life. We seek to find a focus around which the varied interests of our lives can be brought together into dynamic harmony. We look with hope at each step toward the building of an organization which is inclusive of the various nations of the world and which will provide a manner of existence for the nations together, so that international problems may be solved.

Yet even as we hope and work for these things we have a certain realization that organization in and of itself is not a complete answer to the problem of man's life. At best we may think of organization as machinery, and we know that there is still needed an animating spirit, even as a locomotive needs steam, or a jet airplane needs burning fuel. At worst we realize that an organization can be seized and manipulated by the unscrupulous. We must acknowledge that neither the Egypt of the ancient Pharaohs nor the Rome of the emperors constitutes our real ideal even though those forms of organization seemed to be very successful in accomplishing the aims of those who established them. Therefore, it may be that once again we are pointed to look at yet another level upon which the analysis of the problem of human life can be made and where the solution can be suggested.

SIN

This further analysis of the problem of human life states that it is sin. This is the analysis which is found in the Bible. Essentially the Bible represents the point of view of the Hebrew people rather than the Greeks or Romans. While the Hebrews did not fail to speak about wisdom and to make efforts at organization, most of all they looked at man in his relation to God and described man's situation as that of a being involved in sin. This is also the way in which modern theologians speak of the matter. It has perhaps not been so popular to think and speak in this way for some time past, but again now, in view of the grave difficulties confronting the world, we find that we are returning to the Bible and reading its words on this subject with a new appreciation of how true they are of life as it really is. One recent writer has said, "For years it has been unfashionable to discuss the problem of 'personal sin.' It was not a respectable subject. That all was not perfect in a bewildering world might have to be admitted, but our failures were but the birth-pangs of an advancing civilization. Life's evils would gradually disappear when financiers had found the solution of our economic problems, when we had a finer education, and higher wages, and decent housing. Lord Passfield has assured us of the 'inevitability of gradualness' and in time all would be well. The preacher hesitated to speak from the text, 'The heart is altogether evil and desperately wicked' (Jer. 17:9). He was on safer ground in a discussion on Freud's psychology and the 'inferiority complex!' Today we know where we are. There is no evil of which the undisciplined heart is not capable; no barbarism that has been perpetrated by man since time began is greater than the horrors that have been unleashed by so-called civilized man during the last few years."[1]

In the analysis of man's problem as sin it is observed that man is fallen. If we describe man's situation as that of being ignorant, then we conclude that if he does something which is not right, he just did not know any better. If he is fallen, however, that means that he might have done better. I excuse myself when I say: If I had only known. I acknowledge my responsibility when I say: I knew better than I did. The story of Adam and Eve in the book of Genesis, symbolic as it is of the situation of mankind altogether, indicates that from the beginning man was faced with choice and, though he knew better, chose wrongly. The etymology of the word "sin" suggests the same thing, for both in Hebrew and in Greek it means "missing the mark."

Man is also estranged. The fact is not just that there is some organization which we have not yet developed, but that there is a fellowship from which we have already departed. Man has a sense of an essential relationship to the ground of his being from which he has himself someway broken away in his own pride and willfulness.

Because man is fallen and estranged he is also guilty. To describe the causes of our difficulties as ignorance and maladjustment is to tend to excuse ourselves. I did not know any better; I was in an unfortunate situation, we say. But to speak of man as being fallen and estranged is to suggest that at least in some way man has lost something which he had and which he might have kept. Although in the classical world, ignorance and lack of organization seem to have been considered the chief causes of the evils besetting man, there was also even there a sense of historical fate and guilt. In history a factor of wrongdoing enters, and then cannot be gotten rid of. It stays on as guilt and works itself out in fate. Gyges slays the king of Lydia, takes his queen and throne, and all seems to go well. But five generations later the guilt of the ancestor is paid for as his descendant loses throne and kingdom. Tantalus slays his son and carries the guilt of this deed as he stands up to his chin in water which eludes his lips every time he seeks to quench his burning thirst. Thus classical tragedy recognizes the problem of man, although it does not know the answer.

As we read the Bible on the plight of man we find it set forth that sin is universal. It is said that sin came into the world through one man, that is, through Adam, and it is shown that disastrous consequences followed upon all because all men sinned. To be a human being, therefore, is to be part of the great family of mankind and to participate in the common lot thereof. Since I am human I am capable of doing whatever man does. I am capable of doing whatever I am capable of imagining. I may even do the very worst when I think I am doing the very best.

At the same time, we see also in the Bible that sin is ultimate. Ignorance is primarily a lack of knowledge about things. Lack of right organization is chiefly a matter of maladjustment in relationship to persons, both others and ourselves. But to describe man's situation as that of sin is to describe it in terms of relationship to God. Thus in Psalm 51 the cry is raised, "Against thee, thee only, have I sinned . . ."

Precisely here in the Bible, however, where the situation of man is viewed most seriously, it is also viewed most hopefully. Just because man as a sinner is fallen, estranged, and guilty in the sight of God, there is wonderful hope. God, the eternal one, will lift the fallen, reconcile the estranged, and forgive the guilty. Thus we are pointed to the solution of salvation as the ultimate answer to the need of man at the profoundest level of that need.

VI

The Travail of the World

Not only the individual person but also the whole world is, according to the Bible, in need of redemption. "We know that the whole creation," says Paul, "has been groaning in travail together until now . . ."[1]

THE PAIN OF THE WORLD

As the Apostle declares, there certainly is much pain in the world. Some of the factors involved are the following. There is the unconcern of nature. Long ago, according to the book of Job, the seven sons and three daughters of that righteous man were together at a dinner in the eldest brother's home, when a great wind came across the wilderness, struck the four corners of the house, and caused it to collapse upon them, bringing death to them all. Tornadoes still sweep across the country. Tornadoes have the force that collapses a house like kindling wood. Tornadoes proceed without any evidence of concern for what is in their path. The labor of a lifetime may be there. Jesus said that God sends the rain upon the just and the unjust. He was speaking of this as an instance of the generous impartiality of God, who is not small and picayunish to bring one thing upon one person and one thing upon another, but even so it means also that when the rains continue and the snows melt and the floods come, they, too, sweep down upon both the good and the bad.

A farm may be inundated and its family perish in swirling waters which are quite deaf to their cries. This is the unconcern of nature.

There is the predatory life of animals. In the book of Job there is a fine portion of the poetry in which it is asked:

"Can you hunt the prey for the lion,
    or satisfy the appetite of the young lions,
when they crouch in their dens,
    or lie in wait in their covert?"[2]

The way animals hunt is wonderful, and the instincts which guide them on their missions are remarkable. But what is described here is also a struggle for existence in which only the fittest survive. The stronger prey on the weaker. The swifter overtake the slower. The more cunning overcome the less cunning. In this aspect the law of the jungle seems like a cruel law. There is no place in it for pity, no room for mercy. The sensitive poet speaks therefore of "Nature, red in tooth and claw." Professor Tillich tells about standing upon a breakwater with a famous psychologist whom he had often heard give lectures on the patternfulness of nature. On this occasion, however, a school of small fish swam frantically in toward the beach pursued by some larger fish, they in turn pursued by yet larger fish. It was a perfect example of aggression, flight, and anxiety. Dr. Tillich says that his companion burst into tears and cried out, "Why are these beings created if they exist only to be swallowed by others?"[3] The law of nature seems to provide for the continuance of the species, but to have little concern for the individual. As Tennyson also put it, "So careful of the type she seems, so careless of the single life." Schelling, who had the feelings of a poet as well as the thoughts of a philosopher, said, "A veil of sadness is spread over all nature, a deep, unappeasable melancholy over all life." The melancholy which man often feels within himself was, to Schelling, the ground of man's sympathy with nature. "For in nature too," said Schelling, "the deepest ground is melancholy. Nature, also, mourns for a lost good."[4]

We have to notice also the existence of disease in creation.

Job, to mention the same person again, was afflicted with loathsome sores from the sole of his foot to the crown of his head, and he took a potsherd with which to scrape himself, as he sat among the ashes. This was a broken piece of pottery such as we pick up in such great numbers in Palestine, and Job's affliction was so grievous that he used this instrument to try to mitigate the torture of it by another torture. Why must there be leprosy in the world? Why must there be elephantiasis, poliomyelitis, carcinomatosis? Why germs? What good is a virus? What good end is served by the common cold? These things are insidious in their attack. We are told that in Cairo almost all the children get polio, being exposed to it in the very early years of their life. By the time they are three or four years old those that have survived have immunity which lasts the rest of their lives. But in San Francisco there is such good sanitation that, on the average, people do not develop a comparable immunity until they are thirty. So—you get better sanitation to take care of disease problems, and yet you expose yourself more than ever to the disease by having been so cleanly! How devastating are the results of disease we know if we have watched a single person waste away from incurable illness.

The transmission of defects is also an element in this picture of creation groaning together. A sociological study of two contrasting families has often been cited. Out of 1,394 descendants of Richard Edwards and Elizabeth Tuthill in the last 300 years, 265 have been college graduates, 100 lawyers, 100 clergymen, 80 public officials, 65 professors, 60 physicians, 60 authors, 30 judges, 12 college presidents, 3 congressmen, 2 senators, and 2 presidents. Among the great names were Jonathan Edwards, Aaron Burr, Eli Whitney, Bishop Vincent, Grover Cleveland, U. S. Grant, Edith Carow Roosevelt, and others. The other family studied over the same period of time was that of the Jukes. Out of 1,220 members, 300 died in infancy, 440 were destroyed by disease, 310 were professional paupers, 60 thieves, 50 prostitutes, 7 murderers, and 53 other criminals.

There is the unequal incidence of death. Some are like Isaac, who breathed his last, and died and was gathered to his people, "old and full of days."[5] Others are like Schubert, who passed away at 32, and left an *Unfinished Symphony*. In India the life expectancy a few years ago was 22, then 27, then 32, but that is still pitiably brief in comparison with our favored situation.

There is the suffering of the innocent. If in all of this of which we have been speaking, there were an apportionment proportional to character or behavior there would seem to be justice in it. If such things come upon one who deserves them, that is one thing; but if in spite of deserving to have them I escape them, and they fall upon someone who does not in anywise deserve it, then where, we ask, is the justice in this world in which we live. The disciples asked Jesus about this in relation to a man who was blind from birth! "Who sinned, this man or his parents?" Jesus answered flatly that sin did not account for this tragedy. "It was not that this man sinned, or his parents."[6] Neither one! And how could it be that these things are balanced out rightly when we think of little children lost in war, or a family wiped out in an auto collision in which a drunken driver is unharmed and unscathed. Illustrations need be multiplied no further to convince us that Paul is speaking the plain truth when he says that the whole creation groans in travail up until now.

CHRISTIANS ARE INVOLVED

It must also be pointed out that the Christian is himself involved in the creation which groans until now, and he is therefore concerned on his own account as well as on account of others for a redemption that has to do with all creation. The involvement of the Christian in the travail of the universe is stated plainly by Paul in the context of the passage we are studying: ". . . and not only the creation, but we ourselves, who have the first fruits of the Spirit, groan inwardly as we wait for adoption as sons, the redemption of our bodies."[7]

This was certainly illustrated in the personal experience of Paul himself. As far as nature is concerned, he not only saw the beauties of the Mediterranean world but also was exposed to the violent acts of nature which are known there. He was in danger from rivers, in the wilderness, and at sea, as he mentions in his correspondence. One memorable shipwreck is described in the book of Acts, but more times than that Paul suffered the same disaster in the waves. As far as animals are concerned there is a somewhat enigmatic reference in one of his Letters in which he says, ". . . if, humanly speaking, I fought with beasts at Ephesus."[8] Was the Apostle at one time actually put in the arena? We know full well that human combat with wild animals was practiced in the Roman Empire. Or was Paul only using a figure of speech?

Disease also seems to have smitten Paul. The "thorn . . . in the flesh"[9] which he mentions has occasioned much discussion in the effort to ascertain exactly what is meant. Perhaps it was recurrent malaria. Writing to the Galatians, he tells them it was because of a bodily ailment that he preached to them at first. Malaria contracted or aggravated in the lowlands of Asia Minor might have caused him to leave the coast and go up into the highlands. Or the affliction might have been ophthalmia or another disease of the eyes. Also in writing to the Galatians, he says that they would have been glad to pluck their eyes out and give them to him, which sounds as if some trouble of the eyes were his problem. Other surmises as to his illness have included epilepsy and arthritis. At all events, whatever its precise nature, disease was evidently something with which Paul had to contend.

As for the suffering of the innocent, we have but to recall that Paul urged those to whom he wrote to obey the Roman authority and was himself a loyal citizen, yet he was ultimately beheaded by a Roman sword on the Ostian Way outside the city of Rome. So Paul certainly illustrates in his own experience what he states in his words, namely, that the whole creation is filled with pain and that even as Christians we are still within this creation and thus must often ourselves groan within ourselves.

THE BRINGING FORTH OF SOMETHING BETTER

The statement of the Apostle is not only a realistic description of things as they are in the whole creation; it is also an intimation of the emergence, through pain, of something better. That the creation is groaning in travail must signify that something new is being born. Mysterious beyond our comprehending as must be the providence of God, yet even to our limited understanding these positive aspects of the present state of the creation appear: The creation even as it now exists is educative. Nature continues its regular course and in that regular course the winds blow and the floods come. But only because of those great regularities, disastrous as is their impact sometimes, do we learn anything in the areas of meteorology and related sciences. We have spoken of the apparent unconcern in nature. But if there were what humanly speaking might be called concern, that is, if upon occasion when a person was in the way, a tornado changed its path and went another way, it seems little likely that we could ever learn anything about the great patterns of meteorological events. So perhaps it is a vast educative process which is going on here, and the pain of which we have spoken is in part at least the pain that is unavoidable in that process. Even in school there are assignments that are difficult and disciplines that are burdensome, and perhaps in similar fashion we should look upon the world that now is as the training ground for humanity.

If this is correct, then the present state of things in the creation may also be considered to be evocative. It calls forth man's best effort to do something about it. As is well known, Toynbee has written world history in terms of challenge and response. Without challenge both societies and individuals often grow soft; to challenge both societies and individuals often respond with remarkable endeavors. Even disease, blighting as it is, constitutes a challenge and evokes the response of scientists who give their lives to the purpose of its conquest. When Jesus spoke of having faith as a grain of mustard seed and thereby being able to say to a mountain to move to another place, did he not suggest attack upon exactly such towering and apparently immovable difficulties as we actually confront in the present world? In his remarkable book *The Faith That Rebels*, D. S. Cairns emphasizes the difference between a faith that acquiesces and a faith that attacks, and insists that the teachings of Jesus constitute the strongest possible call to move against all the things which bring tragedy to life.

And once again, the situation of a universe in travail may be intended to excite our expectation for the future. The very groaning of the world may lead us to look toward what is yet to come forth. "For in this hope," says Paul in the same context, "we were saved."[10] If everything were plain before our eyes already, there would be no reason for hope and no need for hope. As it is, precisely because all is not yet made perfect, we look forward with eager longing toward that which is to be. Perhaps sometime, seen from a better vantage point, even the pain and travail itself will be recognizable as having had its proper and necessary place in the emergence of what has come to be. Alfred Tennyson, whose sensitive response to the pain of the world has already illustrated our thought above, has also expressed the kind of faith to which we here allude:

> Oh yet we trust that somehow good
>   Will be the final goal of ill,
>   To pangs of nature, sins of will,
> Defects of doubt, and taints of blood;
>
> That nothing walks with aimless feet;
>   That not one life shall be destroy'd,
>   Or cast as rubbish to the void,
> When God hath made the pile complete;
>
> That not a worm is cloven in vain;
>   That not a moth with vain desire
>   Is shrivell'd in a fruitless fire,
> Or but subserves another's gain.
>
> Behold, we know not anything;
>   I can but trust that good shall fall
>   At last—far off—at last, to all,
> And every winter change to spring.[11]

And the Apostle Paul said, "I consider that the sufferings of this present time are not worth comparing with the glory that is to be revealed to us."[12]

VII

The Deliverance of the Individual

Because of the plight of man and the travail of the world, we need redemption. The plan of God for the deliverance of the individual, the transformation of society, and the renewal of all things will, therefore, be our next consideration.

THE BIBLICAL VIEW OF MAN

As we turn to the problem of the deliverance of the individual, we note first that the biblical view of man is at once more serious and more hopeful than any other view. As we have seen, the Greek-inspired scientific view of man says that insofar as he is in an unsatisfactory condition, man is ignorant. This is a relative rather than a radical statement of man's situation. True as it is, it leaves us with the opportunity of excusing ourselves. We did not know any better. The view which is like that which the Romans seem to have had, and which is found in the social and psychological sciences, describes man as unorganized. We are lacking in proper organization. This is a provisional rather than a profound description of man's state. True as it certainly is, it still leaves us the opportunity of excusing ourselves. We are not adjusted properly yet. The biblical view can recognize all of the truth in these views, but it also says something that goes beyond them. To recapitulate, the Bible says man is a sinner whose situation includes the following facts.

Man is fallen. If we have fallen from some situation where we were higher and better, then how shall we ever get back up there again? If, above all, in falling we have injured and damaged ourselves, how shall we be able to climb as high again?

Man is estranged. He has broken away somehow from God. If we have broken away from a relationship, with the ground of our being, if we have become someway separated from a fellowship with God, how shall that ever be restored? If a piece of paper is torn in two, how can you ever put it back together again? Man is guilty. He is himself responsible for the pride with which he has turned away from his Maker. If one has the guilt of responsible wrongdoing, how can the guilt ever be removed? Shakespeare's murderer wishes that he could wash his hands in all the oceans of the world and yet he feels that that would not suffice and they would all be reddened by the hand he would thrust into them.

This is the very serious description which the Bible gives of the situation of man who is just not ignorant and unadjusted, but has someway gotten away from his God.

At the same time that the Bible is so terrifically serious about man's situation it is also more wonderfully hopeful than anything else. The other views of which we have spoken, important as they are, thrust us back upon our resources. We must learn and become more intelligent. We must get ourselves organized. And these things, it would appear, we must do all by ourselves, or else be lost. The Bible is more profoundly and wonderfully hopeful than that because it tells us that we do not have to do these things all by ourselves. And it tells us that by telling us the story of Jesus Christ.

Jesus worked in our midst in order to help us. It is said that when he was born Joseph was told to give him the name of Jesus because that means "savior"—"he will save his people."[1] When Jesus himself began his work he said that he came to seek and to save the lost. The point of his teaching almost all the way through was that of finding what was lost, recovering what was misplaced, retrieving what had gone astray, receiving back him who had gone away. Jesus' associations were of this sort. He

was known as the friend of publicans and sinners. The purpose
of his death was this—to give his life as a ransom for many.
The Bible tells us, then, that somebody has come amongst us
whose purpose is to be of help to us.

It also tells us that God has a plan for us. That plan is to
help mankind and to answer the need of mankind. We can believe that because we know about Jesus Christ and what he did.
If our God were but a vast cosmic force, incomprehensible to
us, moving in an impersonal way in the vast reaches of the universe, we might still be lost mites upon a speck of dust of a
planet, but according to what Jesus has made us know about
God, God is concerned for us. He cares about us. According to
what Paul has to say, which he learned from Christ, we are all
in need but God has set forth a plan of salvation. It is the Christian message and it is good for all. "All have sinned," said Paul,
but "they are justified by his grace as a gift."[2] So the biblical
view is more serious than any other view of man, but it is also
at the same time more wonderfully hopeful.

Andrew Gillies, the fine Scots preacher, somewhere tells about
a British scholar and religious leader who was approaching the
end of his life. His had been a distinguished career. Now his task
was at an end. Everybody felt that he had been a saint. He had
been unselfish, he had been kind, he had been an inspiration
to multitudes of people. He had performed an enormous work
in the field of Oriental scholarship. Yet when a friend slipped
in to see him and tried to tell him what a saint he had been, he
raised a hand and said, "Don't say that. I'm a sinner looking
to God for mercy." And Dr. Gillies commented: "Exactly so.
The world knew of his achievements, of his victories, of his ultimate attainments. He knew how far short he had fallen from
what he longed to be. He knew of the inner conflicts with the
lower self, fighting for supremacy; of the days when he had
miserably failed to be the man he wanted to be; of the long years
of weary struggle necessary to arrive at the point he had reached;
of the unattained and unattainable ideals which haunted his
soul even in the hour of the dissolution of body and spirit. And
knowing all that he laid no claim to the title of saint."[3]

That is at once the radical seriousness of man's situation realistically assessed, and at the same time the wonderful hopefulness with which man may look to God for his mercy.

THE PLAN OF SALVATION

Next we may affirm that the plan of salvation is greater than the problem of man. One is not utterly discouraged by a problem if there is a plan for coping with it. Above all, if the plan is bigger than the problem, then one can work on the problem hopefully. As made known in the Bible, the divine plan of salvation may be comprehended under three "r's." The first "r" stands for regeneration. The problem is that man is fallen and the answer is that regeneration is possible. "You must be born again," said Jesus, according to John 3:7 (Phillips translation). Man is born in a natural way, but he must also be born in a spiritual way. He must undergo a renewal of his spiritual self. Nicodemus, to whom Jesus said this, did not see how this could be possible. It seemed preposterous to him. Obviously you cannot go back and be born all over again. How nice that would be, if you could start out once again as a fresh and innocent baby and do everything all over again. You cannot do that, says Nicodemus. But the word which Jesus used had a double meaning.

In the Greek it is a word which means "again" but also means "from above." It is translated in the Revised Standard Version "anew." A birth from above is possible, and that birth is at the same time a renewal. It gives a person a fresh start. Is it true? Did it ever happen? Harold Begbee wrote a book called *Twice Born Men,* and another one called *More Twice Born Men.* This has happened to some people with spectacular suddenness. It has happened to others with gentle gradualness. But in either case it is there as part of God's answer to man's problem, that man may be born again, anew, from on high.

The next "r" stands for reconciliation. If there is estrangement how can it ever be overcome? According to the Bible it can be done, it is done, and God is there doing it all the while. If there is misunderstanding and estrangement between people, sometimes it is the person who has really been the one wronged who has to take the first step. According to the Bible that is what God is doing all the while. He is taking the first step to restore the relationship with man: ". . . God was in Christ reconciling the world to himself . . ."[4] He has given us the message of reconciliation: ". . . be reconciled to God."[5] If a piece of paper is torn in two, as far as I know, it cannot be put together again, but if a bar of metal is broken, it can be welded and the welded part may be stronger than any other part. The place that once was broken but was bonded together again, in fiery heat, holds now better than any other place. Thus, in Christ, God has re-established the bond with man.

The third "r" in the biblical plan of redemption stands for remission. We spoke of man as having a sense of guilt. Our situation is not just that we are ignorant and do not know any better; it is not just that we are not well enough organized yet and do not have enough clubs and associations to make everything run smoothly. Our situation is that of pride and rebellion against God and consequent guilt in relation to him. How can that be removed? How can that ever be washed away? According to apostolic testimony, God has done something about this, too. In this connection Paul refers to the mercy seat.[6] In the Old Testament the mercy seat was the gold lid on the ark of the Jewish people. On the Day of Atonement blood was sprinkled on it, and thus the mercy seat stood to them for a way in which the wrongdoings of the year could be wiped out. Paul uses that same word and says God has put Christ forward as that. Like the mercy seat he is a means by which guilt is removed.

So there they are: regeneration, and reconciliation, and remission—the three "r's" of the Bible which outline the divine plan of redemption. As we use these words we cannot escape the feeling that they stand for matters greater than we can easily comprehend. Perhaps it is as it was at the end of the Civil War when the Emancipation Proclamation was signed. It is said that in the Southland a group of Negroes was gathered at night around a fire of burning pine knots to pray for freedom. Into their midst came a man bearing a copy of the Emancipation Proclamation. He read it to the people, but they were ignorant and could not comprehend the meaning of the words they heard. They looked at him in stupidity and lack of comprehension. Then half in anger and half in tears the messenger crumpled the paper on which the Proclamation was written and flung it over their heads crying, "You're free. Black men, you're free." Then an old mammy took up a plantation hymn, "I'm glad salvation's free." Only then did they catch the meaning of what they had been told. Even so, the words we have been using may exceed our comprehension, but they say to us that we are free.

WHAT MUST WE DO?

Redemption is offered, yet even so it is not always easy to accept it. In his book on *The Grandeur and Misery of Man*, David E. Roberts told of a person for whom life was empty and intolerable. This person believed that God forgives other people, but he was not able to find the sense of forgiveness for himself. Dr. Roberts ventured to suggest that in this case straining was mixed with evasion, for one would have to be a very unusual person to be the only member of the human race whom God could not forgive. "May not this feeling of being unparalleled and in a class by himself be what my friend cannot yet relinquish?" asked Dr. Roberts. "His sense of worthlessness is so interwoven with a feeling of self-importance that he cannot yet find the blessedness of his true worth in God's sight." "The main point," the writer went on, "is that you and I cannot create God's forgiveness toward this person. Nor can the individual make it real by conscious decision. Yet, the relationship is already offered from God's side; and if my friend ever undergoes, in his own way, a meeting upon the Damascus road, the important change will occur not outside, but inside. His grip upon this odd mixture of self-hatred and self-importance will finally be broken, and he will enter effectually into a relationship he has known about, from a distance, for a long time."[7] The acceptance of redemption is as radically difficult and as amazingly simple as that.

To help us make the acceptance, certain steps are mentioned in the Bible. Confession is one of these, namely, the affirmation of belief and trust in Jesus Christ through whom God has made the redemption possible. ". . . if you confess with your lips that Jesus is Lord and believe in your heart that God raised him from the dead, you will be saved."[8] Baptism is another step, and this is the undergoing of a symbolic act which signifies repentance and renewal. "Repent, and be baptized every one of you in the name of Jesus Christ for the forgiveness of your sins; and you shall receive the gift of the Holy Spirit."[9] Entrance into the fellowship of reconciliation is yet another step. Those who accept the offer of God's friendliness are bound together with him and also with one another. As the recipients of the kindness of God they extend the hands of kindness to one another. Thus the word "fellowship" is prominently used of the earliest Christian church, and of the company of believers it is said, "And the Lord added to their number day by day those who were being saved."[10]

VIII

The Transformation of Society

In the preceding chapter we discussed the deliverance of the individual, and now we turn to the problem of the transformation of society. The first thing which must be emphasized is that the two things go together. The changing of persons in their individual lives and the changing of society in its corporate nature are matters mutually interrelated.

INDIVIDUAL AND SOCIETY

For one thing, the deliverance of the individual is hindered by an untransformed society. The soul does not work very well in a starving body. Fasting is a spiritual exercise sometimes employed, but if half the world goes to bed hungry every night the results must be more harmful than beneficial for the soul. Carlyle once said, "It is not because of his toils that I lament the poor, but what I do mourn is that the lamp of his body should go out; that no ray of heavenly or even earthly knowledge should visit him, but only in the haggard darkness, like two specters, fear and indignation."[1] If people are starving, then there is fatigue and susceptibility to disease, lassitude and enervation, bitterness of spirit and the presence of anxiety and resentment. This is why, to cite a single example, when Mr. Samuel Higginbottom went to India as an evangelistic missionary, and saw the life being slowly squeezed out of the people by long continued starvation, he turned around and came back to study at an agricultural school and then returned to India and established the notable institute of agriculture at Allahabad.

The soul does not work very well in a slum environment. There are occasional wonderful exceptions where great people come out of very underprivileged backgrounds, but on the whole it is statistically true that in a blighted area there will be a disproportionate amount of crime and disease. A relatively small proportion of a city's population will be housed there; a relatively large proportion of the city's problems will originate there. This is why Jacob Riis went into the slums of New York City to do his life work. This is why Jane Addams founded Hull House in an underprivileged part of the great city of Chicago.

The soul does not always survive continual temptation. No doubt some of the tests that come to us are for our strengthening, but there are also temptations which society unnecessarily throws in the way of its weakest members which are terribly destructive. Here is a man for whom alcoholism is a disease. To him the sight or smell of drink is almost overpowering. He knows that he has gotten himself into a position where his family and his work are both in jeopardy, yet everywhere he turns in his work somebody offers him a drink. One longs therefore for a reordering of society, at least to the extent that those who so proudly claim for themselves the right of individual liberty to do what they want to do, would grant a comparable right of individual liberty to others not to do what they do not want to do, and would not bring upon them the insidious and persistent pressures which some are unable to resist. This is why Alcoholics Anonymous constitutes so effective a group. They are people who know what this problem means from the inside, and they band together to provide an environment in which somebody else can be helped rather than harmed. It is certainly true that the deliverance of the individual is hampered if society is not transformed.

The other part of the picture is that if an individual is delivered then he wants to transform society. If an individual receives the wonderful deliverance of the Christian gospel, then he knows about Jesus Christ and naturally, knowing him, he has at least something of his attitude. Jesus had indignation against wrong, courage to stand against it, courage to assist those harmed by it; and the one who is redeemed by him must necessarily have some such attitude. He who knows Christ, knows how the Lord valued and counted precious the personality of every individual. He likewise, then, must be thoughtful of the precious personalities of people, harmed and blighted as they are by evil forces in the world. This is why Walter Rauschenbusch wrote about how his eyes were hot with unshed tears when he saw the poor exploited for gain. This is why William Blake, mystic though he was, of whom one might have thought that he would have withdrawn from the world, wrote instead:

> I will not cease from mental fight,
>   Nor shall my sword sleep in my hand,
> Till we have built Jerusalem
>   In England's green and pleasant land.[2]

These two things go together—the deliverance of the individual and the changing of society.

THE BASIS OF HOPE

Next we will affirm that Christian salvation is our great hope for the changing and transforming of society. Hope has often enough been placed in other things, things which may indeed have that place but which are not enough. Evolution has been our hope. In the nineteenth century it was doubtless our most real hope. We had discovered the fact that plants and animals, and probably people too, are going through a long process of development. In their struggle for existence there is an adaptation to environment in which the fittest survive. Accordingly it appeared reasonable to conclude that the best kind of people, living in the best kind of society, is what would ultimately come out of the process. It is surely not wrong to think that in the long process of development going on in the world we can trace something of the purpose of God himself. But evolution by itself is not our sufficient hope, for in the process, as we look at it more closely, there is not always advance to higher types, but there is also stagnation. Are there not some sand worms that have not changed for millions of years? They became so perfectly adjusted to their environment that they stayed permanently in the same condition. There is not only stagnation, but also what we may call "devolution." Sometimes the process goes backward; it runs down instead of climbing up. In the field of art, one often finds the work of creative genius at the beginning; after that comes imitative mediocrity and progressive degeneration until at the end of the line is not a climax of perfection but a low point of poverty-stricken production. Petrie established dating for ancient Egypt on the basis of the deterioration of style in pottery vessels: At first they were made with finely formed handles, but these degenerated until at the end of the sequence there was nothing left but a little ugly wavy line on the side of the pottery. Things can go down as well as up, and that is why evolution by itself is not our sufficient hope.

Even when the process of development does move upward, the accomplishments seem always to be matched by the dangers that emerge. We have increased power for good today, but also increased power for evil; and we can never tell in advance which way it is going to be used. We have increased size and complexity of things, but that is not always an unmixed benefit. As compared with a simple village a great city may not have all the advantages on its side. People are all the time trying to move out of the cities, and then they find that the cities spread and they are back in them. Acceptance of evolution as our main hope also tends to excuse us from doing anything about the matter, if we think that it is an automatic process. Acceptance of it as our main hope likewise tends to put our hope off—may it not be a thousand years or a million years before things will have become perfect? We need a greater hope, though this is part of our hope.

Revolution has been the hope of many people in the twentieth century as well as long before. The disciples of Jesus went into the Roman Empire and it was said of them that they turned the world upside down. That was revolution, and good. Revolutionary struggle marked the beginning of the life of our country, and we think good things came out of it. But revolution as man's main hope has failed us in the twentieth century. It has been the hope of certain great masses of people, but in their experience we see many ways in which revolution may fail. The means may spoil the end. The revolution looks so desirable that any kind of means are used to get it and then to maintain it, and so violence becomes a permanent part of what is established. The system that is set up may be a new system but it may still be the same old kind of people who are operating it, and greed and ambition and rivalry and strife may corrupt it. The system itself may be wrong, contrived too much by human ingenuity, and when revolution becomes reaction it shows itself as not our final hope.

No, it is not the continuance of evolution and not the inauguration of revolution but the extension of salvation which is our deepest and ultimate hope. The extension of salvation means this: Only God can make men really new, and only new men can make a new society. Emil Brunner writes about it thus in his book on *Eternal Hope*: "Before man can really create something new, he must himself be renewed. That such personal renewal can be effected through faith by the Spirit of God is the witness of the New Testament and of Christian experience. This renewal begins at the point where man's own doing never suffices: in relationship with God. . . . Man seeking himself in his own strength becomes the forgiven sinner, whose sin was that he relied upon his own freedom and self-assurance for what God alone can effect. The revolution begins from within, in the heart, and consists in the fact that the independent man becomes the one who is utterly dependent on God; and this is an act in which—what is incredible to the unbeliever—the slave becomes free, the sinner a child of God. The true revolution consists in this innermost transformation, which is wrought through the Cross of Jesus Christ and which means birth from above . . . by the Holy Ghost. The revolutionary character of the Christian faith means: only the regenerate man can create truly new conditions." Dr. Brunner goes on to illustrate his point by contrast with Communist theory.

That theory supposes that if you change the society you will produce a new man. Indeed Brunner recognizes that a new sort of Communistic man is produced by Communistic education, but then the prognosis that is made from the standpoint of Christian faith is only verified: ". . . this new man is only a variant of the old, and the conditions which he creates are only variants of the former ones. Slavery instead of the hoped-for freedom, and instead of justice the new injustice of state pillage; instead of humanity, complete inhumanity. Revolution shows itself to be the worst form of reaction—a lapse into the most primitive tribal organization, into organized sub-humanity."[3] So over all partial hopes and all failing hopes, our real hope is in the extension of salvation, where God makes men new, and where new men make a new society.

RESPONSIBILITY FOR CHANGING SOCIETY

As it is our privilege, therefore, to accept the deliverance of Christian redemption, it is our responsibility to undertake the transformation of society accordingly. It is our responsibility to be concerned. George A. Buttrick has somewhere put it in terms of seeing faces rather than things as we look at life. "There are businessmen who see only things—sales resistance, charts, profits; there are other businessmen who see faces—the faces of those who work for them and the faces of those who have no work. There are statesmen who see only things—battleships, voting booths, newspaper headlines; and there are other statesmen who see faces—faces of the poor, faces of little children, and myriad faces slain in war. There are would-be preachers who see only things—church buildings, card indexes, yearbook figures; and there are other preachers, ordained by a tenderness beyond the hand of man, who see faces—faces wistful and sin-scarred, lonely and brave."[4]

To have a conscience, a Christian conscience, is a part of our responsibility. It is said that John Newton wrote the beautiful hymn "Glorious Things of Thee Are Spoken" when he was traveling on a slave ship, underneath the hatches of which were imprisoned men on their way to a dark fate. Even to horrible evils conscience sometimes awakens slowly. To be a combatant is a part of our social responsibility. Lynn Harold Hough tells about a group of thoughtful men who discussed the question "What is the greatest thing about a man?" One said that the greatest thing about a man is his ability to think. Another one said that it is his ability to decide, his power of will. A third said, "You are both wrong. It is his power to feel. All the great things in life go back to emotion." But finally the fourth in the party said, "None of you has gone far enough. The greatest thing about a man is his capacity to get into a moral fight."[5] W. Gene Berry, of the United Church of Canada's Board of Evangelism, has said recently, "A so-called spiritual experience that does not result in social outreach is the worst of all sins. When we bring men to Christ we must challenge them to social witness. One spiritual problem of our times is a weak-kneed pietism which confuses witness merely with talking about Christ. Witness must also involve acting for Christ, standing up to be counted on great moral and social issues of our time. . . . we shall not truly serve our Lord unless our evangelism has a social content."

And to be Christlike is most important of all. It is told of Mrs. Humphrey Ward that she once wrote a letter to a member of Parliament in England, asking his help on behalf of a needy family in his district. She felt that she could appeal to this great man because of his known interest in social welfare. He was always working for good social legislation. But this member of Parliament wrote back to Mrs. Ward, "I am so busy with plans for the race that I have no time for the individual." Mrs. Ward sadly filed the reply away, but wrote across it this remark, "Our Divine Lord, when last heard from had not attained this sublime attitude!" To be Christlike must mean to be concerned for all of society, but a society that is found in individual people near to us as the man on the way between Jerusalem and Jericho was near to the Good Samaritan. Thus it is our privilege to accept the deliverance that is offered us as individuals, but then it also becomes our responsibility to be concerned for the transformation of society, wherever we can touch it in any single person near to us.

IX

The Renewal of All Things

When we consider the plight of man, who is always someway short of what he wants to be, and when we think of the travail of the world, which is so beautiful in many ways, yet in which the cries of pain arise from strife and trouble, we long for the renewing of everything.

We can accept the deliverance which is offered to us as individuals, that is, God's gracious forgiveness and blessing. And as those who have received these benefits, we can endeavor to be useful in the transformation of society. But there is a limit to how much we ourselves can do to change things.

THE LIMITS OF HUMAN ENDEAVOR

We cannot live long enough to get all our problems solved. Wonderful progress is being made. In the realm of medicine, yellow fever used to be a terrible scourge, but when we went into yellow fever areas a few years ago we received inoculations, which provided protection. Polio is coming under control. It is said that within another twenty-five years more it will be virtually eliminated. As for cancer, only the outer bastions of this dread disease are falling as yet. How long will it be? And for now there are those who hobble in braces and lie in pain. In economics we are learning some of the laws of that realm, and hope for the day when there will be enough for all, distributed well enough that all shall have some. But today there are people still hungry and starving. In international affairs we hope we are learning some of the lessons, and someday surely there will be an international organization, effective enough to guarantee peace. But in our day little children have still been buried in the debris of bombed homes, and refugees have been sent out to wander by millions.

How long will it be yet? It looks as if it would be somewhat longer than we will be here, before everything becomes perfect. As a matter of fact, even if we could hope to live much longer than is now possible, it is not certain that even then we would find everything perfect upon earth. It seems as if we get some problems solved and others show up that we had not been expecting. This happens in life; it happens also in human history. We make developments in beneficial things, and we find that harmful things have also been developed and are likewise more potent and dangerous.

What is evident, therefore, is that we confront in our human life and our human history these inexorable limits of death and of sin. Within the present framework of human life and human history there seems to be no possibility for us by our own power to overpass those limits. We can no longer believe in the myth of inevitable progress, once so widely accepted. The truth about human history is told rather in a biblical parable. A man sowed good seed in his field. While he was asleep, his enemy came and sowed weeds among the wheat. When both wheat and weeds came up, the servants asked the owner what to do about it, and he said that they had better leave the field alone lest in pulling up the weeds they tear out the wheat. But when harvest time came they would separate the weeds from the wheat. I do not know whether this is your kind of gardening or not, but this does seem to be our kind of history. In history weeds and wheat grow together. Not until the final harvest will the definitive separation of them be possible.

NO LIMITS FOR GOD

But there are no limits to what God can do. It is in his power to renew everything. God is able to make us new, and he is able to make our world new. This is prophesied in the Bible. There it is said that God is going to change nature. The time will come when the desert will rejoice and blossom as the rose.[1] God will change animals. The wolf will dwell with the lamb. The leopard will lie down with the kid. The calf and lion and fatling will be together. And a little child will lead them. The sucking child will play over the hole of the asp, the weaned child will put his hand on the adder's den.[2] Even people will behave differently. They will beat their swords into plowshares. They will convert their spears into pruning hooks. Nation will not lift up sword against nation. They will not learn war any more.[3]

There is also a prophetic intimation of the character of the renewed world in the Gospel picture of the birth of Jesus. The Christmas story contains, as David E. Roberts has pointed out, "the vision of a restored humanity and a restored creation." "In it," he says, "we see every level of existence brought into peace and harmony around the babe lying in a manger—the stars in their courses, the animal kingdom of the sheep and oxen, the work of mankind in the shepherds, and the wisdom of mankind in the Magi.[4]

How much of what the prophets say about the desert's blossoming and the wild animals' being friendly together is literal and how much is figurative it may be difficult to tell. Yet it is a fact that in places such as Imperial Valley the desert has come literally to blossom as the rose. And Howard Thurman tells about visiting a home in the Southland where at the door he was motioned to utter silence. He was led to a back window which looked out upon the patio. There was the baby of the family sitting on the lawn, and a rattlesnake had crawled up beside it. The little baby was patting the rattlesnake and the rattler was rolling over happily. They watched transfixed and silent lest a single sound should break the spell. After a while the rattlesnake crawled away. Perhaps perfect fearlessness, perfect faith, perfect love, would reconcile all the antagonisms that rend this world, destroy its unity, and cause trouble to its people. We are led to believe that such a world is possible by God's action, bringing such harmony as that.

We believe in the possibility of such a world not only because the prophets gave us pictures of it but also because Jesus Christ began to make it so. He really began this new world, this renewing of all things. One might follow D. S. Cairns in his book *The Faith That Rebels* and with him look through the eighth and ninth chapters of Matthew for just one place in which to see it. There is the record of many healings which Jesus performed. His hand of blessing was laid upon a leper, his healing was brought to the centurion's servant, to Peter's wife's mother, to the Gadarene demoniac, to the palsied man, to the ruler's daughter who had died they thought, to the woman with the issue of blood, to two blind men, and to a demoniac. Every time when there was faith in the person, or faith in those round about, wonderful blessings came. These were signs, not such as the Jewish people asked for, that is, marvelous portents, but genuine signs in the sense of revelations of the presence of the Kingdom of God. To those who saw them and to those who understood them these were indications that God's Kingdom was already present and already at work and that it was God's will that men should be freed from the limitations of death and sin under which they were bound. "It is surely now perfectly clear," writes Cairns, "that there is one great principle running through all these sayings about faith, that the Synoptic Gospels regard the whole realm of sin within the heart and of tragedy from without which strike at and poison the life of man as not being part of the unchangeable order of God. They are intruders, and since Christ has come, they can be dispelled by faith."[5]

So we believe that God can make things radically new as the prophets pictured, and that Jesus began to make it so already since his coming was the coming and the beginning of God's Kingdom. Therefore we do have a hope for the renewing of everything that goes beyond the limits of death and sin which presently burden human lives and human history.

ULTIMATE HOPE

When we discussed the individual and spoke of how we personally need and do receive God's help, we pointed to three "r's" in the Bible story: rebirth, reconciliation, and remission. Likewise as we confront the limits of human history there are three "r's" in the Bible which express a universal and ultimate hope, transcending those limits. The first is resurrection. Jesus Christ who brought us the beginning of God's Kingdom was still a man. As a human being upon this earth, he too confronted the limitations of human life—sin and death. The sin of other people did its very worst with him and death was the end of his life just like that of every person. He met the worst sin in the world and was slain by it. He died in youthful days, his movement barely started. But the New Testament gives us the word "resurrection." It says that God raised him up. Therefore an individual person may struggle against difficulties in this life, beset by sin and suffering, and fall at last in death, yet have confidence and believe that God's power is able to lift him up into the glory of the beyond. Paul declares that in Christian baptism we share already in the death and burial of Christ, ". . . that as Christ was raised from the dead . . . we too might walk in newness of life."[6] And of the experience of the man of Christian faith Emil Brunner writes: "Life is no longer a journey into death, but into eternal life, and death has now only the significance of a transitional stage on this journey."[7] The doctrine of the resurrection lifts us above that limit which otherwise faces us so inexorably.

The next "r" in the biblical doctrine is return, the return of Christ. The word for this in the Greek New Testament is *parousia*, and this means primarily "presence." The New Testament expects the presence of Christ in the world someday, in such a widespread, unmistakable, and universal way that it will be like the lightning that is seen in its flashing from east to west. Brunner says: ". . . it is clear that this thought of the future coming is anything but a piece of mythology which can be dispensed with. Whatever the form of this event may be, the whole point lies in the fact that it will happen. . . . Faith in Jesus Christ without the expectation of His Parousia is a voucher that is never redeemed, a promise that is not seriously meant. A Christian faith without expectation of the Parousia is like a ladder which leads nowhere but ends in the void."[8]

The third "r" is regeneration. We have used the word in speaking about the rebirth of the individual, and it is so used in Titus 3:5 in an allusion to baptism as "the washing of regeneration." But in Matthew 19:28 the same word is used in relation to the renewal of the entire universe. There indeed the Revised Standard Version simply translates the term as "the new world." And the New Testament does look forward to such a new world. Paul describes both the whole creation and the individual person as groaning in pain, and anticipates for both a future glory of surpassing wonder: And the seer of Revelation hears a voice which says, "Behold, I make all things new."[9]

Charles W. Ranson has told of taking down off of his bookshelves a volume which was written forty years before by an internationally recognized theologian. It has the title *The Christian Hope,* and it deals almost exclusively with individual immortality. "This," writes Dr. Ranson, "is an essential part of our Christian hope. We are offered in the gospel an assurance which we all crave as we face the inescapable fact of death, for those whom we love no less than for ourselves. But to interpret the hope of the gospel solely in these personal terms is to miss its true grandeur and fullness. The hope of which St. Paul writes in Romans 8 is a hope for the whole creation. Here and elsewhere he looks toward a mighty consummation in which God's final victory will be manifest. Time moves to a terminus. History is not an endless spiral. It has an end. And it is characteristic of Christian faith that this is seen and interpreted both in cosmic and in personal terms. We repeat in the words of the Nicene Creed: 'He shall come again with glory to judge both the quick and the dead. Whose kingdom shall have no end.' We do not know *what* is coming to the world. But we know *who* is coming. It is he who came and lived and died and rose again; who is with us here today and who will meet us at the end. That is the joyous hope in which the Christian lives. This saving hope, in its New Testament meaning, is bound up not only with what God has done—once for all—in Jesus Christ, but in what God will do."[10]

Part Three:

THE REDEEMER

X

He Gave Us an Example

The need for redemption and the fact and hope of redemption have been discussed in the foregoing, and now it is appropriate that we turn to the work of the Redeemer through whom that which we experience and that to which we look forward become possible. According to John 13:15, Jesus said, ". . . I have given you an example, that you also should do as I have done to you." The setting of this saying is that unforgettable scene when Jesus came with his disciples to eat the Last Supper. This group of men had no servant, no slave, so Jesus divested himself of his outer garments, girded himself with a towel, and performed for his disciples the work of a slave in that he came to each and washed his feet of the grime of the dusty Palestinian pathways. Having done so, he said the words we have just quoted. The words can apply not only to the one event but to the whole significance of all that Jesus did and was. It was, therefore, a part of the work of the Redeemer that he gave us an example.

THE PLACE OF AN EXAMPLE

It is extremely valuable to have an example. An example is concrete. People must often think of religion as speculative. They undoubtedly often suppose that it is a set of abstract ideas which may or may not be correct. But in Christianity we really have something to talk about which is tangible, namely, the example given us by Jesus Christ. Such an example is convincing. No doubt people often think of religion as something which is idealistic. It paints a picture, they think, which is pleasant but hardly real. If it were only possible to live this way it would be nice. If it were only possible to have this kind of a world it would be desirable. In fact, however, we are not talking about an ideal suspended in the air but about an actual life lived upon this earth.

This example of which we are speaking is a contemporary thing. In our education many of us were trained in the doctrine of evolution, and we tend to look ahead supposing that what is really good is yet to come. But in this case we are talking about something which is not hoped for a thousand or a million years ahead in the future but about something which has already transpired within the fullness of time of which the New Testament speaks and in which we still live.

THE PORTRAIT

Since Jesus has given us an example, people have often wished that they possessed an actual portrait of him so that they could look at this picture and see exactly what he was like. Thomas Carlyle once said: "I am only a poor man, but I can say in serious truth that I would give one-third of what I possess for a veritable contemporaneous representation of Jesus. Had these carvers of marble chiseled a faithful statue of the Son of man, as he called himself, and shown us what manner of man he was like, what his height, what his build and what the features of his sorrow-marked face were, I, for one, would have thanked the sculptor with all the gratitude of my heart for that portrait as the most precious heirloom of the ages."[1]

But we have nothing like that. The oldest paintings of Jesus that have yet been found are those that are in the catacombs at Rome, and in a house-church of the early Christians at Dura-Europas on the Euphrates River. They are probably at the earliest from the second and third centuries and then on. We have no such thing as Carlyle would have given a third of his possessions to have. But we do have in the New Testament a consistent portrait of the character of Christ. It is true that even in the New Testament there is no complete biography of Jesus. But there is a consistent representation of what kind of person he was and what sort of example he gave us. In point of time as to when they were composed, the earliest part of the New Testament is probably a series of Letters that were written by Paul. They have to do with various practical problems. But if one reads them one begins to see that almost incidentally there is shining through them the portrait of Christ and that every problem is being brought into the light of his presence. Thus we learn many things about the life of Jesus in these Letters that Paul wrote for practical purposes. We learn that Jesus was born a Jew, was descended from David, and had several brothers, one of whom, James, Paul knew quite well. Jesus worked among the Jews rather than the Gentiles. He gave teachings, and Paul quotes some of his sayings. He ate a last supper with his disciples. He died by the Roman method of crucifixion. He was buried. He rose. He was seen by Cephas and others. Above all, there is a definite conception of the character of Christ that shines through these Letters. Paul may be talking about lawsuits, he may be talking about whether women should wear hats in church or not, but sooner or later there shines through, even in the midst of these many minor problems which he had to discuss, the example of the character of Christ. We learn from Paul's Letters that Jesus was characterized by humility, by forbearance, and by a complete absence of self-seeking. These traits are held up for the imitation of Christians and the duty of a Christian can be stated concisely in the words: ". . . put on the Lord Jesus Christ . . ."[2] Now it is true that Paul sometimes says that Jesus did these things according to the Scriptures, and there have been skeptics who have said that he just read the Old Testament and out of it manufactured this picture of Jesus. C. H. Dodd, whose line of thought we have been following at this point, properly asks: "Where will you find in the Messiah of prophecy or apocalypse the moral character which Paul attributes to Jesus as Messiah?"[3] No, you simply do not find this anywhere else; it is the real example of Christ shining through.

The same thing is true of other Letters of the New Testament. Take, for example, Hebrews, which we often think of as a very theological and even allegorical document. But see how much it tells of what Jesus was and did. He was of the tribe of Judah. He preached salvation. He was faithful and obedient to God. He learned obedience by suffering. He was tempted but without falling into sin. He met great opposition. He prayed to be saved from death. He was crucified outside the gate of Jerusalem. He arose again from the dead. Then we come to the Gospels. There most of all we have the portrait of Jesus, yet even there the present-day scholar would say, "This really is not biography as we think of biography now." D. Elton Trueblood has some-where written about the Gospels like this: "Sometimes we voice our regret at our lack of direct knowledge concerning the per-sonal appearance of Jesus. This figure who means most to man-kind must remain forever unknown in many respects. We possess portraits of modern men and busts of famous persons of classic time, but we have no such means of knowing Jesus. Not only are we lacking in an actual portrait, but also in a word portrait, for the four men who left us the best accounts of his life did not think it worth while to tell us how he looked or acted. They did not even leave us a detailed account of his personality, but simply recorded a few of his words and deeds. This failure to portray Jesus more adequately seems, at first sight, a definite loss, and we are sorry that the men who knew Jesus so well did not have our particular interests in mind. But when we think more deeply we realize that the method followed by the Evange-lists is both more satisfactory and more artistic. They tell us much about Jesus unconsciously and describe him indirectly rather than directly."[4]

So it is that while we do not have a statue or portrait of Jesus such as Carlyle wanted, nor even a detailed biography, we do have letters and writings close to his time in which we have a coherent picture of what he was, what he stood for, what he said, what he did, and what he suffered.

THE POWER OF AN EXAMPLE

Consider, then, the power of this example. This compelling example, which Jesus has given us, conveys the power to imitate it, and its influence is passed on from one to another. To the words which Jesus said, let us add now some other words that are found in the New Testament. He said: "I have given you an example, that you also should do as I have done to you." Listen to the next words, those of Paul: "Be imitators of me, as I am of Christ."[5] That is the next link in the chain. Paul has become an imitator of the example of Jesus. Thus he says to other Christians: "Be imitators of me . . ." That this actually happened is shown by what Paul wrote on yet another occasion: "And you became imitators of us and of the Lord . . ."[6] So first we have the example of Jesus, then the imitation of that example by the Apostle, and then the imitation of that example in turn by the Christians, many of them. So the compelling example of Christ has the power to communicate itself so that it is imitated, and so that it is passed on, not just to the great Apostle, but on through him, and on and on. At last it reaches Thomas à Kempis, and his own book, *The Imitation of Christ*, becomes a powerful link in the chain. Yes, the influence of the example of Christ is recognizably present now all around the world. It can be seen in the faces of people and in the deeds of people in many lands. They have heard the message of Christ, they have learned how he girded himself with a towel and bent down and washed the feet of his disciples, and they have become in some degree like him.

In the light of this analysis it is probably fortunate that we do not know many of the external details about the appearance and the manner of Jesus. People might then be tempted to artificial imitation of some part of the manner of life of Jesus; now they are free instead to catch the spirit of his life and be imitators of that. In 1 Peter 2:21 it is also stated that Christ has left us an example, and in this case a unique word is used. F. W. Dillistone comments: "The word used in the passage for 'example' is a most interesting one. This is its only occurence in the New Testament, but in the wider Greek world it stood for one of two things: it might mean the tracing by which children could guide their pens and so gradually form their letters; or it might mean the artist's sketch of a building or the model which needed to be filled in by others. In either case the word represents an outline sketch, not complete in all its details but sufficient in its general form to enable others to proceed with confidence in their task of bringing to concrete expression the example provided for them. This surely suggests a wonderful and most satisfying pattern of Christian living. We are not left without guidance, and yet we are not bound by a rigid code; we are not divested of all responsibility, and yet we are given a rich freedom." [7]

Such are the nature and the power of the example of Jesus. Charles Clayton Morrison has somewhere written: "If a man does not see in Jesus the 'highest, holiest manhood' there is no argument that can convince him. Though one may be convinced that Jesus fulfilled the prophets, and wrought supernatural miracles, and rose from the dead, the belief of all this would not be faith unless one discerns the intrinsic beauty and strength of the moral character of Jesus and responds to it in terms of conduct, choosing to take the risk with Jesus and his way of life rather than to dwell in the tents of materialism and secularism." [8] The example of Jesus is in fact changing people and the world. Having spoken of the New Testament "portrait" of Jesus, we may recall how Whistler was once asked for help in the hanging of a new and beautiful picture. The man who was working with it complained that he could not make the picture fit the room. The great artist looked over the matter, then said: "Man, you are beginning at the wrong end. You cannot make that painting fit the room. You will have to make the room fit the painting." Even so, the picture of Christ has been introduced into a world with which, at many points, it is not congruous. When it is put over against our way of life, and our order of society, it does not fit. We must change the room. We must change the surroundings to conform with the portrait that is brought into the midst of the world in the life of Jesus Christ.

XI

He Taught Us the Truth

Jesus gave us an example. This fact, which we have discussed in the preceding chapter, is stated in the New Testament, and this way of speaking of what Jesus has done for us corresponds in general with the way of looking at Jesus found in the great stream of pietism in the history of Christianity. Jesus, who said, "I have given you an example," said also, according to John 16:7, "I tell you the truth." It was also a part of the work of the Redeemer, therefore, that he taught us the truth. This way of looking at what Jesus has done for us corresponds with the viewpoint of liberalism in Christianity, which has seen Jesus above all else as the teacher of eternal truths.

THE PLACE OF TEACHING IN HIS WORK

Let us ask, then, what place teaching actually had in the work of Jesus. The answer is that it had a surprisingly large place. Popular expectation of the Messiah in his day did not emphasize the teaching role of the one whose coming was expected. Then as now many felt that conditions were too bad for the slow processes of education to suffice for an answer. Rather than for a teacher, men looked for a Son of David who would be a military conqueror, or for a Son of Man who would be a supernatural judge.

The temptations of Jesus show that he himself was tempted

to do things other than just go around quietly teaching and preaching and talking to people. He was tempted to turn stones into bread, which was surely to minister to the economic needs of people; or to cast himself from the pinnacle of the Temple, which was presumably to do supernaturally marvelous things which would cause people astonishment; or to worship Satan and thereby attain the kingdoms of the world, which presumably meant to use political means for world conquest. He did not do any of those things, however, but rather went out and spent much of his time talking to people as teacher and as preacher. Those same temptations may have assailed Jesus later in his ministry. We note times when this may have been the case and at those times particularly we observe that he prayed and then went out and went ahead talking to people, preaching and teaching. When a miracle performed at Capernaum brought great crowds to his residence, he went away early in the morning to pray. Rather than return to Capernaum, he said: "Let us go on to the next towns, that I may preach there also; for that is why I came out."[1] When he fed the five thousand they were about to come and take him by force to make him a king. He withdrew to the hills, and when next we find him he is on the other side of the Sea of Galilee and his first words are: "Do not labor for the food which perishes, but for the food which endures to eternal life, which the Son of man will give to you . . ."[2] He left the place which would provide popular response on a lower level, and prayed, and went on teaching people, preaching to them, and instructing them.

Note also the relatively large extent of teaching materials in our oldest sources concerning Jesus. It is generally held that the oldest sources are Mark and the hypothetical documents known to scholars as "Q" and "L." Mark contains 661 verses, Q is estimated at 270 verses, L at over 400. Mark is mostly made up of narrative of what Jesus did, Q is almost entirely his teachings, and L likewise has many of his sayings and parables. By this evidence, teaching bulked large in his work.

Furthermore, Jesus was recognized by his contemporaries as a teacher. He was called "Rabbi," a title for a teacher, by his own disciples, by interested outside persons, and by the people in general. T. W. Manson remarks: "The fact that He was addressed by His opponents as 'Teacher' is difficult to explain unless He was in fact recognized by them as their equal in point of scholarship. . . . The impression left by the accounts of His dealings with these men is not that they saw in Him a village craftsman turned amateur theologian but rather a competent scholar who had developed heretical tendencies."[3] The recognition which he was accorded by his contemporaries has been granted him also by the world ever since, and the designation "the Great Teacher" belongs to him before all men.

THE NATURE OF HIS TEACHING

Next we turn to the nature of his teaching. It was not unconnected with what went before. He quoted the Old Testament Scriptures and interpreted them. If we look to see what sort of quotations he made from the Old Testament, we find that he quoted from all three main parts of the Old Testament, that is, from the law, the prophets, and the writings. Professor Manson thinks it probable that he knew the Old Testament in Hebrew, and possibly also spoke with the rabbinical teachers in the rabbinical Hebrew used in the schools of the law. He not only quoted portions of the Old Testament, but also uttered sayings similar to some of the sayings of the rabbis, as well as some things taught by other teachers in the religions of the world.

Although the teaching of Jesus was not unconnected with what went before, it may unhesitatingly be called unique. On the religious side, he taught, for example, that God is the Father. This was said in Isaiah, "thou, O LORD, art our Father,"[4] and it was sometimes said by the rabbis, but listen to Claude G. Montefiore, a liberal Jewish scholar of England, as he speaks about the distinctiveness of Jesus' teaching at this very point: "It is apparently a fact that Jesus thought of God as his (and our) Father, and used the term Father for God more habitually and constantly than is the case with any one Rabbi of whom we know. And this regular conception of God as Father, in proportion to the intensity and vividness of the feeling which suggested it, was something which may fitly be called original."[5]

Turning to the ethical side, note that here, too, the teaching stands within the framework of his times, yet is definitely unique. "You shall love your neighbor as yourself,"[6] is a command of the Old Testament and is quoted from there by Jesus. But in the Old Testament the reference is to the people of Israel and a limit is drawn around the teaching at that point. Love your neighbor among your own people. The horizon does not extend farther. Jesus, however, gives the same teaching in such a way that there is no national, racial, or class limitation as to who your neighbor is. His teaching is not only unlimited but also positive. We have found in many religions of the world in some form or other the teaching that one should not do to another what he would not like done to himself. This teaching comes forth in the words of Jesus with unqualified positiveness— to do what you wish men would do to you. Furthermore, his teaching has unity. It is pervaded throughout by one and the same spirit. In his discussion of the originality of Jesus from which we have already quoted, Montefiore points to the comparatively homogeneous body of doctrine all attributed to one man, the unity of spirit, the beauty of form, that which Jesus does not say as well as what he does, and the passion and intensity of the whole, as outstanding characteristics. Then he illustrates what he means about the high originality of the teaching of Jesus by referring to the Beatitudes. "The Beatitudes as a whole seem more than each one taken separately. There is a certain glow and intensity about them which seems new and distinctive. We can find Rabbinic parallels to each of them, but as a whole they seem original. If I be asked, 'In what does the impression left by the Beatitudes in Matthew seem to you peculiar and original?', I find it very hard to put that impression into words. Perhaps it is a feeling as if all religion were concentrated and expressed in a certain condition of soul, which manifests itself in gentleness and pity and love and the patient endurance of wrong; in a certain peacefulness, which is also capable of utmost heroism and sacrifice, in a certain glow and enthusiasm, which produce a peculiar and indomitable happiness.

Before the ideal of this religion all else appears to fade away; all that is external and institutional; all that is civic and political; all that has to do with beauty and knowledge; all that makes for careful and orderly and gradual removal of evils by intelligent forethought or wise legislation; all conceptions of progress. All these things are good and are necessary, and yet the Beatitudes seem to teach the one thing needful which is more needful than any of them, and which goes both before them and after them. The Beatitudes seem to illustrate the unqualified absoluteness of the teaching of Jesus."[7] Thus a Jewish scholar writes about the teachings of Jesus. His teaching is not unconnected with what went before, but it is unique.

And his teaching is understandable. He spoke in everyday language and simple words, and it is written that the common people heard him gladly. Also it is unforgettable. Down across the years man has not been able to get away from it. In form and in content his concise statements, inimitable stories, and remarkable dialogues have made an indelible impression.

THE TEST OF ITS TRUTH

How do we know that what Jesus taught is the truth? For one thing, there is something universal about the teaching of Jesus. To illustrate this point Harry Emerson Fosdick once suggested comparisons with Napoleon and with Michael Faraday. The former was a genius of a peculiar and individual sort, the latter was a revealer of something universal. Concerning the pioneering of the secrets of electricity by Faraday, Fosdick wrote: "He uncovers something universal in the world that always has been here and that men have not known. His greatness is not so much in himself as in what he unveils, something woven into the fabric of the universe from everlasting to everlasting, that you and I can use and our children after us. Thus to reveal the universal is the highest kind of greatness in any realm."[8] What Faraday did about electricity, Jesus did about God. He has revealed universal truth, and that in the very most important of all possible realms.

His teaching is also inescapable. Continuing the comparison

with Faraday, Fosdick also wrote: "Just as soon as Faraday had let loose in the world the meaning of electricity, man could not run away from it. We cannot let loose in the world a force like electricity and then avoid it. Henceforth electricity haunted men. It plucked them by the sleeve. It tapped them on the shoulder, saying, Use me! When once something like that has been unveiled it cannot be escaped. So Christ let loose in this world a kind of life that mankind never has been able to escape."[9]

This teaching is validated not only by its universality and inescapability but also by its verifiableness. It may be tested by experiment. Jesus himself said, ". . . if any man's will is to do his will, he shall know whether the teaching is from God or whether I am speaking on my own authority."[10] That says, Take this teaching, try it, see whether it works or not, and so you will know its truth. Undoubtedly we illustrate what Jesus meant when we take his way and find that it works, and also when we turn away from him and find that the way that is not his does not work.

And this truth is personal. It is embodied in Jesus himself, and finally it is he himself who makes convincing impact upon us. Once more to quote Dr. Fosdick in his eloquent expression of the understanding of Jesus to which this chapter has been given: ". . . ideas are poor things until they are incarnate. Did you ever fall in love with unselfishness? Of course not! Nobody ever falls in love with unselfishness any more than one falls in love with the Meridian of Greenwich. What we fall in love with is not unselfishness but unselfish people. It is when an idea becomes incarnate that it becomes powerful. . . . Our religion is impersonated. Christianity is Christ. And to know him and love him until his spirit is reproduced in us and the Christ of history becomes the Christ of experience—that is vital Christianity."[11]

XII

He Bore Our Sins

In that broad stream of thought in Christianity which may be called "pietism" there is a strong emphasis upon Jesus as our example, and in that other important thought movement known as "liberalism" there is major emphasis upon him as the great teacher. Meanwhile orthodox thought has never ceased to point to the fact that Jesus in some way took our sins upon himself, and this constitutes another aspect of the work of the Redeemer to which we must now turn. One among many statements of this truth in the New Testament is found in 1 Peter 2:24: "He himself bore our sins in his body on the tree..."

SIN CAUSED HIS DEATH

In endeavoring to understand this profound matter we may make a beginning by noticing that sin caused the death of Jesus. In saying that Jesus "bore" our sins, the text just quoted speaks as if sin were a weight. Indeed it is. In individual life when many wrong things are done and many right things are not done, the total result is as if a great burden were pressing down upon one. When Bunyan's Pilgrim first started for the heavenly city, he was weighed down by a heavy burden upon his back, and it was the burden of sin. The world too is weighed down, as it were, by the accumulation of all the misdeeds of the past. Under that weight we are retarded in our progress and hardly know how to move forward. Where could one draw a line in Palestine now, after all the wrong things that have been done on all sides over there, that would be entirely true and fair to everybody? Where can one draw a line in society that will show exactly the responsibility of a criminal as distinguished from the responsibility of his environment and of his heredity? There can be an accumulation of wrong that weighs down upon people and upon the world, and if you are, like Pilgrim, trying to climb a steep ascent, the heavier that weight is the harder the going is.

But if you are going up a mountain the weight which endangers you may be what you have on your back, or a boulder that breaks loose above and hurtles down toward you, or an avalanche that gains momentum and power as it thunders upon you. It was in this latter way that the weight of sin fell upon Jesus. It was not the weight of his own wrongdoing but the weight of the wrongdoing of the world which fell upon him and crushed him. We can see some of what it was. The military power of the Roman Empire was involved. It was a procurator, a governmental official of that Empire, who pronounced the sentence of death upon him. It was the ecclesiastical machinery of the Jewish nation that was involved. The high priest held the first trial. Public apathy and fickleness played their part. Many were not concerned and others may have changed their cries from "Hosanna" to "crucify." There was personal treachery and timidity. One disciple sold Jesus and eleven disciples fled. But this sin that causes the death of Jesus is not just something that is two thousand years behind us. It is a manifestation of what is still to be found in human life. After analyzing the forces which brought death to Jesus in somewhat the same way as I have done, Henry Sloane Coffin then remarks: "This was the world which executed the Life subsequent generations until this hour revere as the best earth has seen. And plainly it is the world in which we still live. All these forces are present and active in our society— religious intolerance, commercial privilege, political expediency, pleasure-loving irresponsibility, unfaithfulness, the mob spirit, militarism, public apathy."[1] And W. R. Maltby has somewhere remarked that "the world is what it is, not because of the superlative wickedness of a few bad men, but because of the ordinary selfishness, prejudice, ignorance, and laziness of mankind—that is of you and me—which has worked up to this sum of wickedness and cruelty."[2] The death of Jesus was caused, then, by sin, and sin is something which is found throughout the world and in all human life. The weight of this fell upon Jesus and caused his death.

HIS DEATH DID SOMETHING ABOUT SIN

Next we may say that the death of Jesus did something about the problem of sin. It is not correct to look upon his death as an event in which he was a passive victim. In dying he was someway dealing with sin and doing something about it.

The death of many people has been due to the sin of the world. War is a manifestation of sin, and hundreds of thousands have died in the wars of the world. Crime is a sin; many lives have been snuffed out by the ruthlessness of criminal behavior. Drunken driving is the same. Many lives have been lost because of the sin of the world. Perhaps every life so lost is a part of the price that has to be paid. Perhaps at last it will be seen that no single life has been lost in vain. Yet there was certainly something special about the way Jesus died, and the death of Jesus has had a special effect upon the problem of the sin of mankind. He died willingly. That is something different from just being caught in the path of an avalanche and having your life snuffed out. There was an aspect of willingness about what Jesus did. He was in some manner or other taking hold of this problem and willingly doing something about it. I do not say that he wished to suffer. He did not, and the prayer at Gethsemane is the indication that he did not. But he willed to do what he did. If it were the Father's will, then it was his will to do it. Now some of us suffer with a sense of inevitability. We are caught. We cannot help it. That kind of suffering does not seem to do much to change a situation, but what Jesus did made a difference. Jesus did die willingly. He set his face to go to Jerusalem. He might have gone to Transjordan or farther away. In the garden of Gethsemane he understood what faced him, and even then still might have gone away. On the cross he refused the drug offered him, indicating that he was still keeping the matter in his own hands. His last words were, "It is finished,"[3] which does not sound like the utterance of a man who was caught in a hopeless circumstance quite beyond his control, but rather like the affirmation of one who was completing an appointed task.

Jesus also died innocently. That again is something different. If we suffer, we are apt to have the uneasy feeling that we had it coming to us. This is a justified retribution. I am not surprised this has fallen upon me; I deserve it. Beside Jesus on his cross were two other crosses with men on them, and one of the men, a criminal, remarked concerning their experience of the same condemnation: "And we indeed justly; for we are receiving the due reward of our deeds; but this man has done nothing wrong."[4] The death of the one on the central cross, who had done nothing wrong, made infinitely more of a difference to the world than the deaths of those other two on either side who after all were being the recipients of the just reward of their deeds. Ralph Sockman imagines that you are driving through a restricted zone where the sign is up that says: "Children at play. Speed 20 miles an hour." But you are late and in a hurry. You are driving fifty miles per hour. Behind a parked car a little girl is at play. She suddenly darts out and into your path. You try to stop but you cannot. You pick up the little broken body and hurry to the hospital. You find out that she is the daughter of a friend. She will live but be a cripple. You have insurance and that will pay the damage, but what about the damage to your conscience? You have to go to the girl's father and ask his forgiveness. And he forgives you because he loves you and knows how sorry you feel, but his forgiveness does not come easily for he loves his little girl and you can see the agony in his countenance even though he manages to overcome his bitterness. Sockman says: "The sight of love that is suffering for the wrongs we have done is the strongest force under heaven to move our hearts to repentance."[5] Now that is exactly what Jesus did for the whole world. He suffered innocently.

And once again he suffered lovingly. He said: "Father, forgive them; for they know not what they do."⁶ Forgiveness of the action of men at such a time is the expression of an amazing love. Also amazing is the loving trust with which, in such a time, he still calls upon God as Father. Lovingly for God because he still cried to the Father at the time. Leslie Weatherhead has somewhere written: "When I see him nailed to a cross and yet looking up into the face of God and calling God 'Father,' I find myself saying over and over again that there are things I cannot understand, there are things which would seem to contradict the loving nature of God; but if Jesus says that God is a Father, and if Jesus can leave his life in the Father's hands, and be certain, by faith, that all will work out well in the end, I can leave my life to him, and I can commit to his capable hands the lives of others, and get them, even in the hour of darkness, to hold on in the dark. The faith of Jesus in God is the lamp which I press to my breast, and its light never goes out."⁷

So Jesus took the impact of sin upon himself and dealt with it willingly and innocently and lovingly. Such action amounted to something different from anything that has ever happened anywhere else. We trust there is at least something of this in every life that has been lost beneath the impact of the sins of the world; yet we are sure that Jesus accomplished something with his death that has not been accomplished elsewhere.

HIS DEATH HELPS US

What Jesus did, therefore, helps us. That is what our text says: "He himself bore our sins . . . on the tree." The things that caused his death are the kind of things that are in our world and in some of our lives. He bore the sins of many. He bore our sins. What he did there has power to change the situation for us. The Bible has several different ways of speaking about this. The statement in 1 Peter that Jesus bore our sins is doubtless based upon Isaiah 53:12, and in the Septuagint translation of that verse it reads: "He bore away the sins of many." This reading reflects the idea of the scapegoat. There was a strange custom in ancient Israel. On the Day of Atonement, the most solemn day of the whole year, they would select a goat and over its head confess the transgressions of Israel. Then they would drive it away into the wilderness of Judea, and as it went it was believed to carry the sins of the people. "He bore away the sins of many." Jesus was like the scapegoat. Sin fell upon him and he carried it away.

Jesus is a ransom. Jesus used this language himself: ". . . the Son of man came . . . to give his life as a ransom for many."[8] This also is a reference to ancient custom. A slave or a prisoner might be set free if someone would pay the necessary price. How wonderful to have the burdensome collar of servitude taken off your neck and to walk again a free man. Jesus has done that for us.

All of these and the other figures of speech found in the Bible to express this matter say to us that Jesus has done something that helps us. Throughout the centuries Christian thinkers have tried to formulate theories by which this matter may be better understood. Gregory of Nyssa felt that the cross was a payment of a debt to the devil. Anselm explained that the cross meant that Jesus had come to be generally one with all mankind and did for man in his crucifixion what man could not do for himself in order to be saved. Abelard saw in the crucifixion the supreme demonstration of the love of God for man. Thomas Aquinas endeavored to harmonize the several theories, but we are told that he finally left his *Summa Theologica* unfinished and, having worshiped at the foot of the cross, cried: "That which I have seen today makes all that I have written seem as trash. I shall not write another word."

While even the most notable theological formulations undoubtedly fall short of expressing the full significance of the death of Jesus, a simple illustration out of everyday life may convey something of the meaning of the fact that he gave his life for us. Thus William Adams Brown has somewhere told about a remarkable surgical operation performed many years ago in New York City. It was, as far as known, the first case of a successful blood transfusion. The life of a baby girl, only a few days old, was ebbing away from an internal hemorrhage.

As a last, and at that time desperate, expedient they attempted a transfusion. The father's arm was laid bare for six inches and an artery extracted. With great care this was connected with a vein in the baby's leg, and the blood began to flow from the one to the other. Those who were looking on saw a dramatic scene. The child was very white, to all appearances already dead. But then a faint tinge of pink appeared on the edge of the ear, a glow spread over the whole body, the fingers and toes brightened, and the lips opened to emit a hearty cry. "That was literally a case of purchase with blood," said Dr. Brown.

So it is that Jesus has not only given us an example and taught us the truth, but has also given his life for us. He has himself borne our sins in his body on the tree. This, difficult as it is to comprehend and express, is an indispensable part of our understanding of the work of the Redeemer. The narrative of what he did in this regard occupies a large proportion of the Gospels, and the explication of the meaning of the death of Christ is the object of much of the writing of the Apostles. In the light of this New Testament emphasis, we can understand how orthodox Christianity has always pointed to the death of Christ as of supreme importance, and to the acceptance in faith of what he has thereby done for us, as basic to the Christian life.

According to this understanding, all else falls into its proper place when we make our start at the cross. "The Christian," writes Lesslie Newbigin, "is one who has forever given up the hope of being able to think of himself as a good man. He is forever a sinner for whom the Son of God had to die because by no other means could he be forgiven. . . . He is [henceforth] seeking to do one thing and one thing only—to pay back something of the unpayable debt of gratitude to Christ who loved him as a sinner and gave Himself for him. And in this new and self-forgetting quest he finds that which—when he sought it directly—was forever bound to elude him, the good life. . . . How ready we are to take Christ as our pattern and teacher only, using the words of the Gospel, and yet never allowing ourselves to face the experience of forgiveness at the foot of the Cross— the humiliating discovery that, so far from our being like Jesus, there is literally no hope for us at all except that He has forgiven us. There is a whole universe of moral and psychological difference between saying, 'Christ is my pattern, and if I try I can be like Him,' and saying, 'I am so far from goodness that Christ had to die for me that I might be forgiven.' The one is still in the world of legalism, and its centre of attention is still the self. The other is in the world of grace, and its centre of attention is another to whose love it is our whole and only aim to give ourselves. The one must always lack what the other increasingly has, the spontaneity and whole-heartedness that come when there is the whole force of an emotionally integrated life behind action."[9]

XIII

He Brought Us Life

In our consideration of the work of the Redeemer we have endeavored to see with the insight emphasized in pietism that Jesus Christ gave us an example, with the understanding stressed in liberalism that he taught us the truth, and with the testimony maintained in orthodoxy that he bore our sins. Now, in agreement with the experience of a multitude of humble Christians, let us turn to the realization that he brought us life. "I came," said Jesus, according to John 10:10, "that they may have life..."

SPIRITUAL LIFE

It will no doubt be agreed generally that it is spiritual life which Jesus Christ brings us. What is spiritual life? Physical life is the life of the bodily organism in relation to its physical environment. We breathe in air, we eat food, we sleep and rest, we rise and walk and work. This is physical life. Mental life is the life of the mind in relation to everything that one can think about. We can hear people speak, we read newspapers and magazines, we think our own thoughts, and we encounter the thoughts of other people. This is mental life. Spiritual life then must be the relationship of the spiritual part of the person to the spiritual environment. In terms of philosophy that would be a relationship to what is true and beautiful and good, and in terms of theology it would be the relation of the soul to God in whom we live and move and have our being. Spiritual life cannot be seen. Spirit is invisible. But one cannot fail to recognize what Paul calls the fruits of the spirit which are love, joy, peace, patience, kindness, goodness, faithfulness, gentleness, and self-control.

Why do we need spiritual life if we already have natural life? The fact that we are here indicates that we have physical life, and the fact that we think indicates that we have mental life. Why do we need anything more? Why do we need what it is here being said that Jesus brings, namely, spiritual life? Because natural life is incomplete without spiritual life. We can see this whether we look at the evolution of the whole universe or at the life of an individual person. In the evolution of the entire universe, as far as we can get a picture of it, we see that there is matter which physics deals with and life which biology deals with and then a realm of values which philosophy and religion deal with. Only when we reach that realm of values do we find the meaning of the whole process. In the development of a person, man can perhaps live as a physical organism and as a thinking person without anything more, but is someway never quite satisfied to do so. Sometimes indeed he tries to limit himself to such things, but usually then he becomes wearied and the result is boredom and sometimes disgust. Man does not live by bread alone. Natural life is incomplete without spiritual life.

Again, natural life goes badly without spiritual life. Natural life would be described by Paul under the term "the works of the flesh."[1] Out of the list of fifteen items which Paul gives, note just one group of three: strife, jealousy, and anger. These, says Paul, are a part of the works of the flesh. They are expressions, therefore, of life that is not qualified and not controlled by spiritual life. Let these attitudes—strife, jealousy, and anger— become the characteristic attitudes of a person and almost inevitably it begins to affect his physical life itself. The natural life does not go well when the spiritual life is not right. I was a student in Germany at the time when Hitler began to reorganize the life of that country and when Goebbels began to administer the bureau of propaganda. Later I read that the people who worked in his bureau of propaganda suffered an unusually high incidence of insanity because they were dealing all the time with lies, falsehood, hatreds, and the mind itself did not work well in such an environment.

Natural life is benefited by spiritual life. I think it was Stanley Jones who once remarked that if mankind would live according to the teachings of Jesus man would rise up free of half of his sickness and woe. What about the other half? We might still have the other half left but, even so, much of its terror would be gone, for it bears upon us most heavily only when we take it wrongly, with bitterness, or with a sense of guilt. Yet spiritual life should not be spoken of as if it were just a means of making natural life better. Actually those who have known most about it have considered that spiritual life is most valuable in and of itself. To know something that is beautiful is worthwhile quite regardless of whether what is beautiful has some monetary or material value. To know the truth, to know goodness—these things are of value in and of themselves. Supremely then, as the mystics all would testify, to know God is supremely valuable.

ABUNDANT LIFE

It is also abundant life that Jesus brings us. "I came that they may have life, and have it abundantly."[2] What is abundant life? Abundant life is overflowing life. It is the kind of life which, as compared with the plain and ordinary level of living, means something more than sufficient. The psalmist knew something of it when he said, "My cup overflows."[3] Jesus' words about good measure could apply to it: ". . . good measure, pressed down, shaken together, running over . . ."[4]

Why do we want abundant life? Because there are different degrees of aliveness. We may be alive more or less. We vary in the keenness of our perceptions in hearing and seeing. In part this is due to variations in the physical organism, and some experiences handicap in this regard. Yet we vary perhaps even more because of the way we handle the faculties we have. Who would not say but that Helen Keller, quite deprived of many ordinary channels of perception, has been more sensitive to the beauty of the world than some of us who have all our faculties? There is a story about an American Indian in New York City. Standing on Fifth Avenue, with the roar of the traffic about him, he heard the sound of a cricket. Surely enough, over there behind a brick, was a cricket making its little chirp. The Indian's keen sensitivity picked this up in the midst of all the noise. Now this is the way it is with life. We vary in awareness and sensitivity, and we vary accordingly in the abundance of life which we experience. People differ in the amount of traveling which they have the opportunity to do, yet some people stay right at home and in interest and in knowledge are citizens of the world. Some tourists, on the other hand, travel widely but, wherever they are, simply play the same game of bridge they would have played at home, and complain if they are unable to find the same kind of apple pie which they would have eaten at home. There are different degrees of awareness of things round about us, and we want abundant life because we want to live as fully as possible.

Does spiritual life mean abundant life? There is an idea abroad that the life and teachings of Jesus are narrow. Nietzsche thought the virtues of Jesus were negative. Swinburne said of Jesus, ". . . the world has grown grey from thy breath."[5] Jesus did say, "The gate is narrow and the way is hard, that leads to life." Some have thought, therefore, that Jesus' way must mean narrow, cramped, restricted, and inhibited life. But there is a law of life in the teaching of Jesus as he speaks about the narrow gate and the hard way. Some of you are going to school. It may seem like a narrow gate and a hard way. It may mean sacrifice for you or for your parents. But you believe it is going to lead to a broader life than you can have any other way. Some of you are practicing voice or a musical instrument. It is hard to keep the practice hour. But if you become able to sing or play gloriously it will be worth all the effort. Some of you are learning a language, and that is hard work. But you may be in another country some day and then you may have the freedom to read and talk at least a little bit with the people of that country. Some of you are taking time to pray and read the Bible every day. Only so can you draw closer to God. In everything that is worthwhile there is a narrow gate to go through, to enter into abundance of life.

But the life which Jesus brings us is also eternal life. In the Fourth Gospel, from which we have already quoted the saying of Jesus, "I came that they may have life, and have it abundantly," one finds that the word "life" is repeated over and over again. About half of the time the word "eternal" is used with it.

What is eternal life? Here is a definition of it from the Greek lexicon: ". . . the life of the kingdom of God, the present life of grace and the life of glory which is to follow."[6] That is a very good definition, because as one reads the Gospel according to John with its report of the teachings of Jesus, one sees that the kind of life of which he speaks is life of such quality that it is already now a part of the Kingdom of God, and therefore it goes on through the portal of death.

Why do we want eternal life? If we have spiritual life and abundant life, need we be concerned whether it is eternal? Yes. Spiritual life is life that is concerned with truth and beauty and goodness, and if these values have no permanence, they have no value at last. A scientist has said, describing the attitudes of his fellow scientists: "They would like to feel that this enterprise of life upon which we have embarked without any volition on our part, is a worthwhile process. They would like to think of it as something more than an endless procession of life out of and into the dark."[7] Surely this is true for us all. If the values we seek are just to be snuffed out some day and that is to be the end, it is difficult to resist the conclusion of a cynical thinker of long ago who concluded that all is vanity. Abundant life is life in fullness, but the fullness of life which man wants as always goes beyond any particular time limit. When he was seventy-seven years old the artist Corot said: "If the Lord lets me live two years longer, I think I can paint something beautiful." Always the goal we seek is just beyond our reach. As a present-day thinker has put it: "While our bodies are the natural prey of death, our minds and spirits already have started on a road that has no visible terminus."[8] Eternal life as well as abundant life and spiritual life is that which we seek and desire and that which Jesus brings.

Notes

Part One: REVELATION

CHAPTER 1. THE WORD OF GOD

1. Genesis 1:3, etc.
2. Exodus 4:22, etc.
3. Genesis 15:1, etc.
4. 1 Samuel 9:27, etc.
5. John 1:1, etc.
6. Job 12:13.
7. Psalm 147:5.
8. Isaiah 55:8.
9. Alfred Noyes, *The Book of Earth* (The Torch-Bearers, II) (New York: Frederick A. Stokes Company, 1925), pp. 325-326. Quoted by permission.
10. Samuel N. Kramer, *From the Tablets of Sumer* (Indian Hills, Colorado: The Falcon's Wing Press, 1956), p. 74.
11. Psalm 33:6.
12. Hebrews 11:3.
13. Romans 4:17.
14. 2 Samuel 7:4.
15. 2 Samuel 24:11.
16. 1 Kings 6:11.
17. 1 Kings 17:8.
18. H. D. A. Major, T. W. Manson, and C. J. Wright, *The Mission and Message of Jesus* (New York: E. P. Dutton and Co., Inc., 1938), p. 677.

19. Revelation 15:2.

20. Paul Tillich, *Systematic Theology*, I (Chicago: The University of Chicago Press, 1951), pp. 117-118.

21. Nathaniel Micklem, *Ultimate Questions* (London: Geoffrey Bles, 1955), p. 18.

22. Exodus 3:2-5.

23. Elizabeth Barrett Browning, *Aurora Leigh*, Seventh Book, lines 821-824.

24. Exodus 34:29.

CHAPTER 2. THE WRITTEN WORD

1. Psalm 119:105.

2. Mark 7:13.

3. 2 Peter 1:21.

4. *Encyclopaedia Britannica*, XI, 14th ed. (1929), p. 128.

5. Quoted by H. Wheeler Robinson, *Inspiration and Revelation in the Old Testament* (Oxford: The Clarendon Press, 1946), p. 193.

6. Alexander Gilchrist, *Life of William Blake* (London and Cambridge: Macmillan and Co., 1863), pp. 192-193.

7. *Ibid.*, p. 194.

8. Percy Bysshe Shelley, *Essays, Letters from Abroad* (London: Edward Moxon, 1852), pp. 41-42.

9. *Ibid.*

10. Amos 3:8.

11. Jeremiah 1:4, etc.

12. Franz Werfel, *Hearken Unto the Voice* (New York: The Viking Press, 1938).

13. Ezekiel 3:8.

14. Job 36:26.

15. Robinson, *op. cit.*, p. 189.

16. Burnett Hillman Streeter, *The God Who Speaks* (New York: The Macmillan Company, 1936), pp. 59-60.

17. H. H. Rowley, *The Relevance of the Bible* (London: James Clarke & Co., Ltd., 1941), pp. 42-43.

18. Jeremiah 23:36.

19. Tillich, *op. cit.*, pp. 9, 11.

20. Genesis 12:1.

21. Exodus 32:11.

22. Isaiah 10:5, 15.

23. Psalm 118:23.

24. Emil Brunner, *Revelation and Reason* (Philadelphia: The Westminster Press, 1946), p. 85.

25. William F. Albright, *From the Stone Age to Christianity* (Baltimore: The Johns Hopkins Press, 2nd ed., 1946), p. 47.

26. Micklem, *op. cit.*, p. 16.

27. Origen, *De Principiis*, IV, 6.

28. Rudolf Bultmann, "New Testament and Mythology," *Kerygma and Myth*, ed. Hans Werner Bartsch (London: S. P. C. K.), I (1953), p. 36.

29. *Ibid.*, p. 42.

30. Helmut Thielicke, "The Restatement of New Testament Theology," *Kerygma and Myth*, p. 155.

CHAPTER 3. THE WORD MADE FLESH

1. John 1:3.
2. Psalm 19:1.
3. Matthew 5:45.
4. Job 1:19.
5. John 1:5.
6. Psalm 150:1-2.
7. H. Wheeler Robinson, *Redemption and Revelation in the Actuality of History* (New York: Harper and Brothers, 1942), p. 168.
8. Reinhold Niebuhr, in *Religion in Life*, XXIII, 3 (Summer 1954), p. 338.
9. John 1:9.
10. Justin Martyr, *Apology*, I, 46.
11. John 1:11.
12. Deuteronomy 14:2.
13. Isaiah 10:20.
14. Tillich, *op. cit.*, p. 143.
15. John 1:14.
16. Isaiah 41:8-9.
17. Isaiah 53:3-5.
18. Tillich, *op. cit.*, p. 143.
19. Emil Brunner, *The Mediator* (London: The Lutterworth Press, 1934), p. 228.
20. Genesis 1:1.
21. John 1:1.
22. Major, Manson, and Wright, *op. cit.*, p. 678.
23. Gustaf Aulén, *The Faith of the Christian Church* (Philadelphia: Muhlenberg Press, 1948), p. 217.
24. Rudolf Bultmann, *Theology of the New Testament*, I (New York: Charles Scribner's Sons, 1951), p. 9.

25. William Manson, *Jesus the Messiah* (Philadelphia: The Westminster Press, 1946).

26. Matthew 11:27=Luke 10:22.

27. Brunner, *Revelation and Reason*, p. 112.

28. Major, Manson, and Wright, *op. cit.*, p. 680.

29. Aulén, *op. cit.*, p. 213.

30. Quoted by Aulén, *ibid.*, p. 212.

31. D. M. Baillie, *God Was in Christ*, 2nd ed. (London: Faber and Faber Ltd., 1948).

32. 1 Corinthians 15:10.

33. Micklem's reference is, of course, to Galatians 2:20.

34. Micklem, *op. cit.*, pp. 102-103.

35. Brunner, *The Mediator*, p. 160.

36. Major, Manson, and Wright, *op. cit.*, p. 685.

Chapter 4. THE WORD OF PREACHING

1. Amos 1:3, etc.

2. Matthew 5:22, etc.

3. Cf. above, p. 28.

4. Romans 10:13; Joel 2:32.

5. Romans 10:14.

6. 2 Timothy 4:2.

7. Acts 6:4.

8. Acts 15:35.

9. Cf. Richard Heard, *An Introduction to the New Testament* (New York: Harper & Brothers, 1950), pp. 30, 139, 229.

10. Paul Hutchinson, "The Onward March of Christian Faith," *Life*, Vol. 39, No. 26—Vol. 40, No. 1 (December 26, 1955), pp. 43-44.

11. James 3:1 ff.

12. 1 Corinthians 1:23.

13. 1 Corinthians 1:24-25.

14. Tillich, *op. cit.*, p. 159.

15. 2 Corinthians 3:5-6.

Part Two: REDEMPTION

Chapter 5. THE PLIGHT OF MAN

1. Angus Watson, in *Treasury of the Christian World*, ed. by A. Gordon Nasby (New York: Harper & Brothers, 1953), No. 885.

Chapter 6. THE TRAVAIL OF THE WORLD

1. Romans 8:22.
2. Job 38:39-40.
3. Paul Tillich, *The Shaking of the Foundations* (New York: Charles Scribner's Sons, 1948), pp. 82-83.
4. Quoted by Tillich, *ibid.*
5. Genesis 35:29.
6. John 9:2-3.
7. Romans 8:23.
8. 1 Corinthians 15:32.
9. 2 Corinthians 12:7.
10. Romans 8:24.
11. Alfred Tennyson, *In Memoriam*, LIV.
12. Romans 8:18.

Chapter 7. THE DELIVERANCE OF THE INDIVIDUAL

1. Matthew 1:21.
2. Romans 3:23-24.
3. Andrew Gillies, in *Treasury of the Christian Faith*, edited by Stanley I. Stuber and Thomas Curtis Clark (New York: Association Press, 1949), p. 622.
4. 2 Corinthians 5:19.
5. 2 Corinthians 5:20.
6. Romans 3:25. The word employed by Paul is used for the mercy seat in the Greek translation of Exodus 25:17, and in the New Testament it is translated "expiation" in the Revised Standard Version.
7. David E. Roberts, *The Grandeur and Misery of Man* (New York: Oxford University Press, 1955), pp. 35-36.
8. Romans 10:9.
9. Acts 2:38.
10. Acts 2:42, 47.

Chapter 8. THE TRANSFORMATION OF SOCIETY

1. Thomas Carlyle, in *Treasury of the Christian Faith*, p. 663.
2. William Blake, *Milton*.
3. Emil Brunner, *Eternal Hope* (London: Lutterworth Press, 1954), pp. 62-63.
4. George A. Buttrick, in *Treasury of the Christian Faith*, p. 664.
5. Lynn Harold Hough, in *ibid.*, p. 678.

CHAPTER 9. THE RENEWAL OF ALL THINGS

1. Isaiah 35:1, King James Version.
2. Isaiah 11:6-8.
3. Isaiah 2:4.
4. Roberts, *op. cit.*, pp. 19-20.
5. D. S. Cairns, *The Faith That Rebels* (New York: Richard R. Smith, Inc., 1930), p. 76.
6. Romans 6:4.
7. Brunner, *Eternal Hope*, p. 111.
8. *Ibid.*, pp. 138-139.
9. Revelation 21:5.
10. Charles W. Ranson, in *The Pulpit* (April 1956), p. 7. Copyrighted by the Christian Century Foundation and reprinted by permission of *The Pulpit* from the issue of April 1956.

Part Three: THE REDEEMER

CHAPTER 10. HE GAVE US AN EXAMPLE

1. Thomas Carlyle, in *Treasury of the Christian Faith*, p. 42.
2. Romans 13:14.
3. C. H. Dodd, *History and the Gospel* (New York: Charles Scribner's Sons, 1938), p. 66.
4. D. Elton Trueblood, in *Treasury of the Christian Faith*, p. 102.
5. 1 Corinthians 11:1.
6. 1 Thessalonians 1:6.
7. F. W. Dillistone, *Jesus Christ and His Cross* (Philadelphia: The Westminster Press, 1953), p. 118.
8. Charles Clayton Morrison, in *Treasury of the Christian Faith*, p. 89.

CHAPTER 11. HE TAUGHT US THE TRUTH

1. Mark 1:38.
2. John 6:27.
3. In Major, Manson, and Wright, *op. cit.*, p. 303.
4. Isaiah 63:16.
5. Claude G. Montefiore, in *The Hibbert Journal* (October 1929), p. 104.
6. Leviticus 19:18.
7. Montefiore, *op. cit.*, p. 109.

8. Harry Emerson Fosdick, *What Is Vital in Religion* (New York: Harper & Brothers, 1955), p. 38.

9. *Ibid.*, p. 39.

10. John 7:17.

11. Fosdick, *op. cit.*, pp. 42, 43.

Chapter 12. HE BORE OUR SINS

1. Henry Sloane Coffin, *The Meaning of the Cross* (New York: Charles Scribner's Sons, 1931), p. 34.

2. W. R. Maltby, in *Treasury of the Christian World*, p. 332.

3. John 19:30.

4. Luke 23:41.

5. In a radio sermon (March 10, 1957).

6. Luke 23:34.

7. Leslie Weatherhead, in *Treasury of the Christian Faith*, p. 133.

8. Matthew 20:28.

9. Lesslie Newbigin, *Christian Freedom in the Modern World* (London: Student Christian Movement Press, 1937), pp. 84-85.

Chapter 13. HE BROUGHT US LIFE

1. Galatians 5:19.

2. John 10:10.

3. Psalm 23:5.

4. Luke 6:38.

5. Algernon Charles Swinburne, "Hymn to Proserpine."

6. G. Abbott-Smith, *A Manual Greek Lexicon of the New Testament* (New York: Charles Scribner's Sons, 1922), p. 196.

7. Quoted by Fosdick, *op. cit.*, p. 227.

8. *Ibid.*, p. 229.

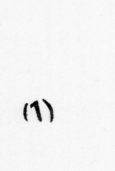

(1)